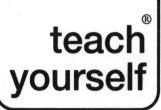

teach yourself

emotional intelligence

D0273591

emotional intelligence
christine wilding

Launched in 1938, the **teach yourself** series
grew rapidly in response to the world's wartime
needs. Loved and trusted by over 50 million
readers, the series has continued to respond to
society's changing interests and passions and
now, 70 years on, includes over 500 titles,
from Arabic and Beekeeping to Yoga and Zulu.
What would you like to learn?

be where you want to be with **teach yourself**

For UK order enquiries: please contact Bookpoint Ltd, 130 Milton Park, Abingdon, Oxon, OX14 4SB. Telephone: +44 (0) 1235 827720. Fax: +44 (0) 1235 400454. Lines are open 09.00–17.00, Monday to Saturday, with a 24-hour message answering service. Details about our titles and how to order are available at www.teachyourself.co.uk.

For USA order enquiries: please contact McGraw-Hill Customer Services, PO Box 545, Blacklick, OH 43004-0545, USA. Telephone: 1-800-722-4726. Fax: 1-614-755-5645.

For Canada order enquiries: please contact McGraw-Hill Ryerson Ltd, 300 Water St, Whitby, Ontario L1N 9B6, Canada. Telephone: 905 430 5000. Fax: 905 430 5020.

Long renowned as the authoritative source for self-guided learning – with more than 50 million copies sold worldwide – the **teach yourself** series includes over 500 titles in the fields of languages, crafts, hobbies, business, computing and education.

British Library Cataloguing in Publication Data: a catalogue record for this title is available from the British Library.

Library of Congress Catalog Card Number: on file.

First published in UK 2007 by Hodder Education, part of Hachette Live UK, 338 Euston Road, London, NW1 3BH.

First published in US 2007 by The McGraw-Hill Companies, Inc.

This edition published 2007.

The **teach yourself** name is a registered trade mark of Hodder Headline.

Typeset by Transet Limited, Coventry, England.
Printed in Great Britain for Hodder Education, an Hachette Livre UK Company, 338 Euston Road, London NW1 3BH, by Cox & Wyman Ltd, Reading, Berkshire.

The publisher has used its best endeavours to ensure that the URLs for external websites referred to in this book are correct and active at the time of going to press. However, the publisher and the author have no responsibility for the websites and can make no guarantee that a site will remain live or that the content will remain relevant, decent or appropriate.

Hachette Livre UK's policy is to use papers that are natural, renewable and recyclable products and made from wood grown in sustainable forests. The logging and manufacturing processes are expected to conform to the environmental regulations of the country of origin.

Impression number   10 9 8 7 6 5 4 3 2
Year   2012 2011 2010 2009 2008

contents

dedication

To my publisher, Victoria Roddam, who had the idea for this book. With thanks for your constant help and support.

Also, for Oliver, already the most emotionally intelligent person I know.

introduction

The purpose of this book

By reading this book, you are starting out on a journey which, if you follow it through, will change your life comprehensively. You will become happier, more confident, get along better with others, and you may well become more successful at work. If you are a parent (or work with children), you will have the chance to pass the skills of emotional intelligence (EI) on to your children, enabling them to form better friendships, gain greater self-esteem, learn more – and simply improve their enjoyment of life

EI may be a subject you have heard about, or read about in the press, and you perhaps purchased a copy of this book to appease a vague curiosity you have about it. Possibly you already have an understanding of EI – you may have read Daniel Goleman's *Emotional Intelligence: Why it Can Matter More than IQ*, which became a seminal bestseller in the mid-1990s. His book was an elegant explanation and exploration of the ideals of EI, but it was by no means a self-help book.

This book is exactly that.

The skills you will learn

You will first gain a thorough understanding of the meaning and impact of EI, and you will then learn the skills and techniques to develop its characteristics in all areas of your life.

You will find this book user-friendly. I will do my best to avoid jargon (or, if I do need to use some, I will clearly explain what it means in day-to-day terms). At the start of each chapter there will be an outline of what you will learn, and at the end the most important points will be summarized to ensure that you don't miss anything before you move forward. During the course of each chapter there will be a variety of activities for you to consider or test out. These will build on each other, so that your expertise increases as the book goes on.

You will use your own intelligence to decide which and how many of the activities you will find helpful – but ideally, do them all. You have nothing to lose, and may find that you gain more than you had anticipated. However, I am not a fan of too many DIY exercises – for the simple reason that experience and enquiry have told me that most people don't do them! I have therefore tried to create a balance. Much of your learning in this book will come from reading, absorbing and understanding the principles of EI.

EI for your own particular lifestyle

You are a unique individual with your own competences and weaknesses. I have therefore attempted to make the book broad-based enough to cover most of the life areas – such as work, personal relationships and self-development – that you may especially wish to work on. If a chapter doesn't seem to cover what is important to you, while you can leave it out, I suggest you stick with it. The skills you will learn will be reinforced in each chapter of the book – sometimes you simply need to apply the same skills to different situations. Even if you think 'This doesn't apply to me', it is still worth reading through the section.

A model for change

There are various ways in which we can make changes in our minds and our lives.

In order to identify and manage our emotions, we have a variety of positive options to work with. We can develop our thinking skills (cognitive restructuring), we can adjust what we do and how we react, and we can learn new life skills and values. This book will cover all of these aspects of developing your EI to the point where it will positively change your life. Some of you will already be familiar with the cognitive model – which supports the link between what we think and how we feel – and for those of you who are not, you will nonetheless find it very straightforward to work with.

Reaching your goal

By the end of the book you will possess an excellent understanding of EI, and of how it can help you to lead a happier life. Moreover, you will have all the skills you need to keep developing further as an emotionally intelligent person.

Keeping it going

Don't simply read the book and put in on a shelf – keep it by you. Keep it in the kitchen, on your desk, or on your bedside table. Dip in and out of it on an ongoing basis and you will find your life changing consistently for the better.

part one

understanding emotional intelligence

While the concept of emotional intelligence (EI) is an historic one, it has only recently, since the mid-1990s, surfaced as an important indicator of a successful lifestyle. For this reason, many of you will know little about its background and concepts. Part one of this book focuses on helping you to understand firstly what EI is, and secondly why it is so important. You will find many examples of both good EI and the lack of it to help you to fully understand its importance as a life skill and why it is worth developing.

01

emotional intelligence: a first look

In this chapter you will learn:
- to explore the idea of emotional intelligence
- more about its origins
- how developing emotional intelligence will positively improve your life.

What is emotional intelligence?

You can be just about as happy as you make up your mind to be.

Theodore Roosevelt, US President 1901–09

Has it ever crossed your mind to wonder why some people with obviously good brains seem to falter in life, while others, who appear to have little obvious academic intellectual ability, seem to do very well? Have you perhaps felt vaguely frustrated that brainpower doesn't always win the day, as you perhaps think it should?

Have you noticed that certain people, who materially have very little in life, seem happy and fulfilled, full of laughter, surrounded by friends, while their wealthier counterparts complain about the unfairness of life, and spend a great deal of time telling everyone what is wrong with their situations?

Surely, academic, career and material successes are the stuff of happiness? So how can we account for what seem to be discrepancies in how well people do or how happy they are? The answer is **emotional intelligence** (EI) – a way of understanding the emotions of both ourselves and others and learning to control these emotions so that you can choose what you say and what you do, in order to engender the outcome you would like to see.

'It's not my fault'

How often do we hear someone say 'I just couldn't help it' or 'It was completely outside my control' when referring to their actions or verbal responses to a difficult situation? In fact, we can always 'help it', and there is very little that we do – short of a jerk reaction to a tap on the knee or blushing – where we are not in some sort of control. The difference between someone who uses EI and someone who does not is that the emotionally intelligent person will fight to maintain control of their emotions and refuse to allow them to dictate their actions unless appropriate. The person who is not using EI will simply give sway to the emotions, regardless of the outcome (and then, of course, say 'I couldn't help it. It just happened.').

Wishing you had done things differently

How many times in your life have you either thought or said 'I wish I hadn't said that' or 'I wish I had reacted differently'? The answer is probably too many times to count, and that is normal for most of us.

In simple terms, becoming emotionally intelligent will reduce the number of times you will find yourself either thinking or saying such things in future.

Here are the characteristics that Daniel Goleman (author of the bestseller *Emotional Intelligence: Why it Can Matter More than IQ*) suggests make up EI. Read through them and you will see the qualities you will be working to develop.

Self-awareness	Knowing what you are feeling and why.
Self-regulation	Being able to control your emotions, even when circumstances are difficult.
Motivation	Being able to persist in the face of discouragement.
Empathy	Being able to read and identify emotions in others.
Social skills	Being able to get along with others through listening, understanding and appreciating their own emotions.

Your journey towards emotional intelligence

Start your journey towards EI by thinking about your own present ability levels relating to each of these characteristics. Developing EI will equip you to make choices and influence outcomes in all the areas of your life in which you choose to use this skill. Put simply, EI is an ability to get along with both yourself and others.

This can be explained in graphic form:

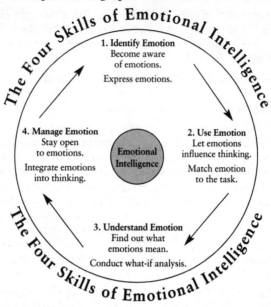

Figure 1

Source: Adapted from David Caruso and Peter Salovey, *The Emotionally Intelligent Manager*, 2004

The following will help you to understand these ideas a little more:

Identifying emotions. The idea is that emotions contain data, signalling to us about important events going on in our world. We need to accurately identify these emotions in both ourselves and others in order to convey and express ourselves and to communicate effectively.

Using emotions. How we feel influences how we think – and what we think about. Feelings direct our attention to important events; they make sure we are ready to take action when required and they enable us to use our thoughts appropriately to problem solve.

Understanding emotions. Emotions are not random events; they have underlying causes. Once we become familiar with these, we can use our emotions to more easily understand what is going on – or is about to go on – around us.

Managing emotions. Because emotions contain information and influence thinking, we need to incorporate them intelligently into our reasoning and problem solving. This requires us to stay open to emotions, whether they are welcome or not, and to choose strategies that include the wisdom of our feelings.

Let's look at Margaret's story:

Case study

The queue at the supermarket check-out was getting longer and longer. Margaret, around eighth in line, could not quite see what was happening, but when a supervisor was called, and the cash register was opened up for investigation, she knew she was in for a long wait. She did feel irritated, but rationalized that there was little she could do, and that it was certainly not the cashier's fault. So, smiling resignedly at the person behind her in the queue, she picked a magazine off the rack beside her and started to flick through it. After a few minutes, she became aware of a great deal of shouting a little further up the queue. Someone near the front was throwing a wobbly at what he termed 'the sheer incompetence and stupidity' of the cashier and supervisor. 'Can't you put this right? Can't you see how huge the queue is? I have to get to an appointment. This is outrageous.' The cashier and supervisor apologized, explained that there was a till problem outside of their control and they were trying to rectify it. They suggested the man go to an alternative till. This led to more, 'Why should I do that? It will lead to even more waiting. This is ruining my evening. I'll never shop here again. I'll be writing to your management about this.' With that, the man left his trolley full of goods and stalked angrily off.

A minute or two after the man had left, three things happened. A further cashier opened the till next door to the defective one, especially for the waiting customers; the broken till sprang back to life; and the supervisor gave Margaret and the others in her queue a £5 store voucher as an apology for the disturbance. Margaret was delighted – not only had she discounted her food shopping, she had picked up two good recipe ideas from the magazine and had a brief but friendly chat with the lady waiting behind her, discovering that they both played badminton at the same club and would meet up again. She thanked the cashier profusely and received a grateful smile. Margaret left the store thinking how well things work out sometimes.

Meanwhile, the angry man had no shopping, no voucher, and he was irritated and angry with the people he was meeting, recounting his 'horrendous' experience. He slept very badly and woke up with a headache.

Begin to use the basic information you have learned already to think about this case study in EI terms.

Which of the characteristics of EI listed earlier can you see used in this story, and by whom? Think about this for a moment before reading on.

Margaret was able to recognize her irritation and acted to defuse it – empathizing with the situation instead of being angry about it, distracting herself with a magazine, and having a brief social chat. Meanwhile, the man ahead of her was completely unable to control his emotions and had little, if any, social skills at all.

This is an example of EI, and the effect it can have on our daily lives.

> *There is nobody so irritating as somebody with less intelligence and more sense than we have.*
>
> Don Herold, writer

Think about the last time you were in a slightly difficult situation. Did you feel that you handled it well emotionally? If not, spend a moment replaying it in your mind. Which of the characteristics that we have been discussing did you lack – and why?

Why haven't I heard of emotional intelligence before?

This is an obvious question for you to ask – and a good one. Are we trying to sell you something that is simply a marketing concept? Are we dressing up 'same old, same olds' to convince you that there is something new out there? On the contrary. Firstly, people have much more emotional awareness now. We simply talk about emotions a great deal more than we used to. Where previous generations learned to 'keep a stiff upper lip' or were told to 'pull yourself together and get on with it', we take a much softer approach to people's emotional difficulties and encourage each other to express how we feel. We have much more awareness of the role that emotions play in the life decisions we make. We have more sympathy when people suffer from negative emotions, such as depression. Once regarded as a fictitious complaint put out by those who were not prepared to get on with their lives, depression is now an accepted medical condition that offers as valid a reason for being away from work as, say, a broken leg – and is also as treatable.

Secondly, the psychological research wasn't there until now. A brief look at its development may be helpful to you.

Our greater curiosity about the human mind

The study of the human mind, while of interest to scientists and philosophers for the last two and a half centuries, has not received attention in the past in the same way that it has over the last 50 years. Sigmund Freud set the ball rolling with his psychoanalytical theories regarding disturbances of the human mind and their causes. He was followed by behavioural theorists and subsequently cognitive behavioural theorists (these two main schools of thought are among hundreds of variations) who offered different explanations of the causes of psychological disturbance but whose goal was – just as Freud's – to relieve people of suffering from any mental disturbance that was having a negative impact on their life. In the case of behavioural theory and cognitive behavioural theory, the relief of such suffering is achieved by teaching people to identify unhelpful beliefs and behaviours, and to replace these using skills and techniques that assist them to get their lives back on track.

However, these psychological therapies focus, in the main, on getting people up the ladder of emotional health from minus 8 (say) back to zero – where zero is the level playing field of life, and a minus number places you in a zone where mental disturbances (such as depression or anxiety disorders) prevent you from enjoying that life.

A more positive approach

American psychologist Abraham Maslow was the first to shift his thinking and research away from studying pathology, and all the ways that people are broken, traumatized and neurotic, towards exploring individuals at their best and discovering what developed the bright side of human natures, rather than the dark side.

In the 1970s, building on Maslow's work, as well as that of American psychiatrist and hypnotherapist, Milton Erickson, Richard Bander and John Grinder (also from the US) developed Neuro Linguistic Programming (NLP) as one of the first theories to suggest that we should not 'stop at zero'. How about getting from plus 3 to plus 10? In other words, don't ignore psychological theory and therapy simply because you aren't 'below the zero line'. Use it as a positive tool to take you even further above it, to a more successful and enjoyable life than you might otherwise have had. Bander's and Grinder's NLP was based on modelling excellence – finding role models who had the personal qualities that you would like to have yourself – and using NLP tools and skills to learn to develop those qualities yourself.

Developing happiness

In the early 1990s, Martin Seligman, a psychology professor from the University of Pennsylvania, published his theories of positive psychology – in a sense, the study of how to be as happy as possible[1]. Without going into a detailed, and open-ended, debate as to what 'happiness' means exactly and how it can possibly be measured, we do have a general acceptance that feeling good about the life we lead is a general goal for most of us, and that perhaps this goal constitutes the nearest we will get to happiness as we understand it. Seligman conducted wide-ranging research that scoured all continents of the world and went back through history in order to attempt to discover an attribute, or set of attributes, that withstood ethnicity, geography, religion and historical bias – in other words, which could globally, and at any time, account for and explain the core traits that would ensure the best chance of lifelong individual happiness.

The emergence of emotional intelligence as a positive quality

In the mid-1990s, the American psychologist Daniel Goleman published a theory he had been developing for some time – again, building on previous theories. His idea was that there was a set of attributes (not dissimilar to Seligman's but more specifically focused), quite unrelated to a person's IQ, that where well developed could have a stunning effect on an individual's personal happiness and professional success. He described these attributes, when placed together, as 'emotional intelligence'[2].

[1] *Learned Optimism*, Martin P. Seligman (1992)
[2] *Emotional Intelligence: Why It Can Matter More Than IQ*, Daniel Goleman (1996)

A brief history of emotional intelligence

- **1930s – Edward Thorndike** describes the concept of 'social intelligence' as the ability to get along with other people.

- **1940s – David Wechsler** suggests that affective components of intelligence may be essential to success in life.

- **1950s** – humanistic psychologists such as **Carl Rogers** describe how people can build emotional strength.

- **1975 – Howard Gardner** publishes *The Shattered Mind*, which introduces the concept of multiple intelligences.

- **1985 – Wayne Payne** introduces the term 'emotional intelligence' in his doctoral dissertation entitled 'A study of emotion: developing emotional intelligence; self-integration; relating to fear, pain and desire (theory, structure of reality, problem-solving, contraction/expansion, tuning in/coming out/letting go)'.

- **1987** – in an article published in *Mensa Magazine*, **Keith Beasley** uses the term 'emotional quotient' (emotional quotient, EQ, is regarded as a measure of EI). It has been suggested that this is the first published use of the term, although Reuven Bar-On claims to have used the term in an unpublished version of his graduate thesis.

- **1990** – psychologists **Peter Salovey** and **John Mayer** publish their landmark article 'Emotional intelligence' in the journal *Imagination, Cognition, and Personality*.

- **1995** – the concept of emotional intelligence is popularized after the publication of psychologist and *New York Times* science writer **Daniel Goleman's** book *Emotional Intelligence: Why it Can Matter More than IQ*.

How does emotional intelligence differ from IQ?

While many of us are only now becoming familiar with EI, almost everyone has heard of IQ, and most people understand roughly what it is measuring. So how is IQ different to EI?

IQ tests were developed around 100 years ago as a way of assessing a person's intelligence. 'Intelligence' in this context means:

- logical reasoning ability
- analytical reasoning ability
- linguistic skills
- spatial orientation.

An IQ test can interpret how well equipped our brain is to learn, retain and recall objective information. It gives us feedback on our abilities to reason well, both verbally and mathematically, to problem solve and to think both in the abstract and analytically.

As a result of this, where an individual's IQ score is high (the average score being around 100), they are likely to be successful academically, hold down good jobs, and succeed in life generally.

As a predictor of an individual's likelihood of a successful life, the IQ test has been the gold standard for a long time. However, it is unable to predict a person's ability to *enjoy* their life, to feel fulfilled and contented – or their ability to do well in life using a completely different set of life skills. In the twenty-first century, these skills – requiring EI as their core – will become a new yardstick for measuring success that includes positive emotions such as happiness and fulfilment.

It's not a question of one or the other

IQ and EI are not competing qualities. They are simply different, and often complementary. It will often be the case that a person with high IQ will possess good EI (and vice-versa, of course – low IQ may often go hand in hand with low EI). No one is suggesting that IQ is not an important, even gold standard, measure of a person's logical and intellectual reasoning, speed and accuracy of calculation, memory recall and visual and spatial awareness. Where IQ has been shown to be weak, however, is in its ability to predict an individual's success in life, where success is a broader concept than pure intellectual achievement.

One point on which both the popular and scientific treatments do agree is that emotional intelligence – if substantiated – broadens our understanding of what it means to be smart.

John Mayer, Psychology Professor,
University of New Hampshire, 1999

Key point: It is a combination of intellectual intelligence and emotional intelligence that is most likely to determine your overall success and happiness in life.

Learning about 'soft skills'

EI is what we call a 'soft skill'. Hard skills are normally distinctly measurable – learned competencies for which we can gain certificates and diplomas to show our exact standard of expertise in any given subject. They usually have a strong commercial value. Most jobs will depend on our ability to show, either through academic work or practical learning, that we are proficient to the standard required in, say, banking, cooking, information technology (IT), librarianship and so on. Learning these skills – while enormously hard work – is relatively straightforward. There are standard routes to learning whichever competency you select. There are graded examinations of your abilities from beginner to expert. There are diplomas and presentations to show that you have achieved your goals and are competent.

Examples of soft skills to help you understand the concept

More and more, in our twenty-first century, ultra competitive lifestyle, the above hard skills are not enough. Employers are also asking for high-quality 'soft skills' such as:

- the importance of getting along well with others
- being an effective team leader (gone are the days when this might be achieved by a carrot and stick approach)
- encouraging the development of others and managing their learning
- self-development
- excellent inter-personal skills
- the ability to use cognitive (thinking) skills to best effect
- being robust in the face of adversity
- an ability to handle criticism and difficult situations positively
- an ability to stay calm in a crisis
- being able to understand and absorb the points of view of others for effective decision making.

These soft skills can be grouped together under the heading of emotional intelligence. Your employer is interested in EI simply because your level of competence in it is good for their business.

Exercise 1

Can you think of a few more 'soft skills' that could be valued in the workplace? Jot them down.

What you have just written constitutes the beginning of some of your own ideas regarding emotional intelligence.

Case study

When John went for a second interview for a new job in IT, he was extremely confident. Although young and with limited experience, he was a straight 'A' student with superb academic and technical qualifications. He felt that his CV 'spoke for him'. His first interview, where he simply had to confirm his specialist competencies, had gone very well.

However, John was quite thrown by the style of his second interview. Instead of asking him questions about his strengths (his superb IT skills), the interviewer was more interested in how he spent his free time, what sort of holidays he took, and whether he did any volunteer work. He asked John to come up with a difficult personal situation that had arisen in the last couple of years and to then explain how he had resolved this. John was asked to hypothesize about facing rejection: 'What will you do if you don't get this job?'; to put forward the names of any role models – people in public life/sport whom he especially admired; and at one point the interviewer seemed determined to deliberately ruffle John's feathers by making one or two critical comments. The interviewer described a hypothetical work problem involving a belligerent client, and asked John to describe how he would deal with this, to get the best outcome.

John was baffled. He could not see what any of this had to do with his IT skills and he felt angry at the way the interview was going. One of John's weaknesses was that he lacked the ability to see what the interviewer was trying to discover. Having taken the quality of his hard skills as being perfectly adequate (as shown in the first interview), the interviewer was now looking at John's 'soft skills'. He was checking out John's emotional intelligence.

How well rounded was John? Did he have self-awareness and other-awareness in all areas of his life, not simply at work? Could he think on his feet if faced with a crisis? Did he have ethical personal goals? How did he get along with others generally?

Could he handle finding himself in an uncomfortable situation and deal with it calmly and maturely? Was he likely to develop the soft competency management skills needed to go alongside his financial expertise in order to benefit the company?

John struggled with this type of interview. He was fortunate to receive feedback that helped him understand that for this organization, self-awareness and self-development meant more than simply taking another exam. He wasn't given the job he wanted, but was in fact offered one (which he accepted) where he would have a chance to learn and develop these skills alongside further IT experience. John was able to build some confidence from this. His firm was investing in him because they saw that, with the right hard and soft skills, he could be a long-term asset to the firm.

Twelve years later, John was still with the same company, but now as a director. He was a good IT expert but, more importantly, he was charming and empathetic, encouraged others in his firm to develop themselves, and he was an excellent role model to everyone who worked with him. He had learned to be emotionally intelligent.

Can I measure my emotional intelligence?

Scientific theory tells us that to properly define a concept, it must be measurable. Frustratingly, EI fails in this regard. There is, as yet, no precise 'pencil and paper' test that can accurately measure a person's EI.

Some might argue that this invalidates EI as an identifiable concept. However, we intrinsically accept many virtues, such as kindness, empathy and wisdom, without having any accurate measurement for them. This neither invalidates them nor diminishes them as qualities that make a great and positive difference in people's lives. EI is simply the outcome of using a group of these qualities.

Do we really want to measure emotional intelligence?

There might even be an argument for not being able to measure EI because of its nature. Can you imagine having a numerical rating for how kind-hearted you are, for instance, against other people? How would you feel if you knew that someone else was several points higher than you on an inter-personal sensitivity scale?

However, if you still want to try to measure EI, there is a variety of books available with titles such as *Test your own Emotional Intelligence* or *Discover your Emotional Quotient*. There is also a variety of companies, accessible on the internet that, in exchange for your credit card number, will offer you a myriad of complex and intricate test questions that will translate into some kind of result. These tests, while purposefully thought out, will lack evidence of any rigorous examination of their accuracy and as such you might question their validity.

For those of you still curious, see the 'Taking it further' section at the back of this book for a list of books and websites that you can check out if you wish to try one of the tests.

The bottom line is that, as yet, there is no empirically researched, scientifically or psychologically validated test for EI in the way that there is for IQ. Indeed, EQ is largely regarded as a marketing concept, rather than a technical term.

While the search continues for such a measure, the complex nature of EI and the qualities it encompasses mean that its assessment to an exact level may always be difficult and inexact. However, the starting point for such a test could be a simple focus on the basic competencies that constitute EI.

Take this informal test to gain an idea of your present emotional intelligence standing

Below is an adapted version of the Boston EI questionnaire, an American model that will give you a basic overview of your skills. Nevertheless, this is an informal test, and will not give you any sort of official EQ at the end; it is just a guideline.

Look at each of the following questions and place a circle around the alphabet letter that most closely relates to your answer.

1 Can you tell when your mood is changing?

   A – always   B – sometimes   C – rarely   D – never

2 Do you know when you are becoming defensive?

   A – always   B – sometimes   C – rarely   D – never

3 Can you tell when your emotions are affecting your performance?

   A – always   B – sometimes   C – rarely   D – never

4 How quickly do your realize that you are starting to lose your temper?

   A – very quickly   B – not very quickly   C – slowly
   D – very slowly

5 How soon do you realize that your thoughts are turning negative?

   A – straightaway   B – quite soon   C – after a while
   D – usually too late

6 Can you relax when you are under pressure?

   A – very easily   B – quite easily   C – hardly ever
   D – not at all

7 Do you just get on with things when you are angry?

   A – usually   B – sometimes   C – Not usually   D – never

8 Do you engage in self-talk to vent feelings of anger or anxiety?

   A – often   B – sometimes   C – rarely   D – never

9 Do you remain cool in the face of others' anger or aggression?

   A – always   B – usually   C – occasionally   D – never

10 How well can you concentrate when you are feeling anxious?

   A – very well   B – quite well   C – just about   D – not at all

11 Do you bounce back quickly after a setback?

   A – always   B – sometimes   C – occasionally   D – never

12 Do your deliver on your promises?

   A – without fail   B – quite often   C – rarely   D – never

13 Can you kick-start yourself into action when appropriate?

   A – yes, always B – yes, sometimes C – not often
   D – no, never

14 How willingly do you change the way you do things when current methods are not working?

   A – very willingly B – quite willingly C – quite reluctantly
   D – very reluctantly

15 Are you able to lift your energy level to tackle and complete boring tasks?

   A – always B – usually C – rarely D – never

16 Do you actively seek ways of resolving conflict?

   A – yes, often B – yes, sometimes C – not often
   D – never

17 To what extent do you influence others about the way things are done?

   A – to a great extent B – to some extent C – very little
   D – not at all

18 How willing are you to act as a spokesperson for others?

   A – very willing B – can be persuaded C – quite reluctant
   D – not at all willing

19 Are you able to demonstrate empathy with others' feelings?

   A – always B – sometimes C – rarely D – never

20 How often do you find that others trust and confide in you?

   A – frequently B – occasionally C – hardly ever D – never

21 Do you find yourself able to raise morale and make others feel good?

   A – yes, often B – yes, sometimes C – rarely D – never

22 How freely do you offer help and assistance to others?

   A – very freely B – quite freely C – reluctantly
   D – not freely at all

23 Can you sense when others are feeling angry or anxious and respond appropriately?

   A – yes, always B – yes, often C – hardly ever D – never

24 How effective are you at communicating your feelings to others?

A – very   B – quite   C – not very   D – not at all

25 Do you contribute to the management of conflict and emotion within your workplace or family?

A – yes, often   B – yes, sometimes   C – rarely   D – never

Give yourself 4 points for each time you circled A; 3 points for B; 2 points for C; and 1 point for D.

Add up the totals as follows:

Total score for questions 1–5   17

This is your self-awareness score

Total score for questions 6–10   13

This is your emotion management score

Total score for questions 11–15   16

This is your self-motivation score

Total score for questions 16–20   17

This is your relationship management score

Total score for questions 21–25   16

This is your emotion coaching score

What this means:

17 or above	pretty good for the start of the book
13–16	some work to do
12–9	a lot of work to do
8 or below	don't despair – try this test again after finishing the book

As you can see, this is simply to give you an idea of those areas in which you may already be EI competent, and of those areas where you need to do more work. Once you have worked through the book and undertaken all of the practical exercises, take the test again. You may be surprised in the increase in your scores.

Can I *really* change my emotional intelligence?

Is EI a developable skill, or is it a more enduring personality trait? The fairest answer is that it is both. Although eminent scientists and scholars continue an ongoing debate on the topic of nature/nurture, the dominance of our genetic inheritance over our ability to learn and change is still an elusive and grey area. It is certainly within an individual's ability to change personal characteristics if they are willing to work hard enough. Our brains are super-computers with a great capacity to learn – and also to unlearn. Most of the literature on EI comes to the same conclusions – that EI is a trait, or set of traits and competencies, that can be developed.

Have you left it too late?

The question of whether a particular stage in our lives is more or less conducive to developing EI is worth considering. There is no doubt that introducing EI skills in childhood has the strongest effect, with a robust body of educational research to back this up (Chapter 12 focuses on how we can develop emotionally intelligent children). We also know that many skills are more easily absorbed and better retained in childhood. This does not mean that as adults we no longer attempt to make changes; rather, we accept that we may have to work harder and for longer to achieve the results that we want.

For each individual, some elements of EI may be easily developed, while others – particularly if they seem contrary to a person's particular basic beliefs and previously developed character traits – might be harder to develop. If you believe – and I hope that you do – that we can achieve most of what we want if we set our minds to it, then EI as a developable and life-enhancing skill will be well within your grasp.

Why bother to develop my emotional intelligence?

In order to make it worthwhile, you need to have some certainty that working on your EI will change your life for the better. To help you decide, firstly ask yourself some further questions:

- Am I always totally motivated?
- Do I always get along well (*really* well) with others?

- Am I a good decision maker?
- Am I able to manage stress, both in myself and in others?
- Do I have good problem-solving skills?
- Would others describe me as empathetic?
- Am I honest and realistic about my own strengths and weaknesses?
- Do I consider how my actions may affect others prior to making changes?
- Am I as successful as I would like to be in my professional life?
- Am I as happy as I would like to be in my personal life?

Unless you have answered 'Yes' to all these questions, your EI could do with some work.

Secondly, read some words from Daniel Goleman: 'Emotional Intelligence counts more than IQ or expertise for determining who excels at a job – any job.'

Thirdly, consider a few pieces of evidenced-based research:

- The Centre for Creative Leadership in the US identified that the primary cause of career derailment among top executives was lack of EI.
- Research into insurance company agents and IT sales representatives showed that those who scored highly on EI were 90 per cent more likely to finish training and double their sales commissions.

Source: Adapted from www.eiconsortium.org

Developing your EI will offer you a chance of increased personal and professional happiness. It will give you confidence and contentment, and an ability to choose and develop the path in life that you most aspire to.

The future of emotional intelligence

I think the coming decade will see well-conducted research demonstrating that emotional skills and competencies predict positive outcomes at home with one's family, in school, and at work. The real challenge is to show that emotional intelligence matters over-and-above psychological constructs that have been measured for decades, like personality and IQ. I believe that emotional intelligence holds this promise.

Peter Salovey, psychologist

(*Emotional Intelligence: Key Readings on the Mayer and Salovey Model*, Salovey, Bracket and Mayer (2004)

Summary

In this chapter you have begun to develop your knowledge base regarding EI, giving you a general concept of what it is and how it has developed.

- One of the problems associated with EI, especially where it is linked to and compared with IQ as though it is an alternative cognitive capacity, is that there is not yet a definitive measure for it, as there is for IQ. However, many unofficial tests will promise you some conclusion, albeit a rather subjective one, if this is of interest to you.
- This chapter has hopefully answered the questions, 'Can I change my EI?' and, if so, 'Is it worth it?' These are the most pertinent questions you can ask if you are to devote further time and energy to this book. The answers to these questions are a very firm 'Yes, you can' and 'Yes, it is'!
- Make a note of anything you feel unclear about, and you will find clarification as you progress through the book.

In Chapter 02 you will learn more about why EI is so important.

02

why is emotional intelligence so important?

In this chapter you will learn:
- the importance of developing EI and the difference it can make to your life
- how much harder life can be without EI
- to understand your emotions and where they come from
- the modern secrets of a successful life.

The advantages of emotional intelligence

We are what we repeatedly do. Excellence, then, is not an act, but a habit.

Aristotle, Greek philosopher

Possessing emotional intelligence (EI) is an important skill. While life will still throw up problems and traumas, EI enables you to deal with these in the best possible way, to make good choices based on wise thinking, and to enjoy great relationships with others.

In simple tabular form, the advantages of EI look like this:

Work : Understanding stress triggers & having more control over reactions to these

Good self-awareness	**Leading to...** **Good self-management**

Personal : recognising the thought processes - eg P + preventing dwelling on the past which I can't change

Acting more assertively at work

Sensitivity to others and their feelings	**Leading to...** **Good relationships with others**

Less self absorbed
More outgoing & relaxed

Being able to move on & establish a new relationship

Exercise 2

Think for a moment about some of the specific advantages that the above might bring you. Jot these advantages down.

How many did you come up with? Here are some further examples – some of which you may have already flagged up.

- **Feeling confident about yourself as a decent human being.** Possessing the skills and character to deal in the best possible way with thoughts and situations as they arise.

- **Being personally competent.** Personal competence is an amalgamation of your self-awareness and your self-management skills. It means that you acknowledge your abilities on the one hand, and use them to your best advantage on the other, producing a good, competent performance.

- **Gaining respect from others and having them simply like you more.** When you act with thoughtfulness and integrity, others will trust you and respect your worth. They will appreciate your honesty and empathy and will enjoy spending time around you. They may even want to be like you!

- **Improved communication skills.** Becoming emotionally intelligent is primarily about getting along well with others. This happens when you are emotionally sensitive to their feelings and emotions, when you can appreciate another's point of view (even if you don't agree with it), when you can express clearly not only your own feelings but transmit an understanding of theirs, and when even serious disagreements can be amicably resolved.

- **Better personal relationships.** Close personal relationships require flexibility and tolerance, acceptance and understanding, as well as the motivation to work hard at making such intimate relationships the best they can possibly be. EI will provide you with these skills.

- **Success at work.** Your EI won't necessary be recognized as such in the workplace. What your bosses will recognize, though, are good communication skills, good teamwork abilities, a positive, proactive approach with creative ideas, and an understanding of the company's ethics and goals. They will appreciate your calmness in the face of adversity, your ability to see all sides of an argument, and your excellent negotiating skills.

How a lack of emotional intelligence is damaging

Put simply, the disadvantages of a lack of EI are the opposite of its advantages.

Exercise 3

Stop and think for a moment about how you might view someone you consider to lack emotional intelligence. What might you say of them? Jot down one or two possibilities.

Here are some examples:

- 'He never appreciates how other people feel.'
- 'She has to be right all the time.'
- 'I hesitate to ask him for a favour, since I know he will be reluctant.'
- 'I find her very hard to talk to about things that are important to me.'
- 'I've never known him put anyone else before himself.'
- 'It's so easy to find yourself in a row with him.'
- 'They're totally inflexible.'

These, of course, are only a few examples. There are many more. However, from these alone we can see how damaging a lack of EI can be to our relationships with others and the negative ways in which others may view us.

A lack of EI is also damaging to our own integrity, and can reduce our own sense of self-worth.

Case study

Jenny had finished work for the day and was looking forward to an evening at the theatre. As she walked back to her car, she noticed one of her colleague's cars parked diagonally across two parking bays. 'How selfish,' thought Jenny. Although there were other spare parking bays, the principle of someone having the gall to do that roused Jenny to anger. 'This person really needs to be taught a lesson,' she thought. Jenny walked back to the reception area to complain. Unexpectedly, the receptionist was not there and Jenny surmised that she had gone home early. This made Jenny even angrier and she took a large sheet of paper from the reception desk and wrote an extremely rude and abusive note about the utter selfishness of the car driver as well as a second note with a scathing condemnation of staff who left their posts before their finish times. Jenny placed the first note on the windscreen of the errant car.

She was so cross about what had happened at work that she was poor company at the theatre and failed to concentrate at all throughout the show – all in all a very unhappy evening.

When Jenny went into work the next day, she discovered her colleagues in a sombre mood. It turned out that, just before Jenny had left the office the previous evening, a colleague backing his own car out of the car park had been struck down with a heart attack, and was now dangerously ill in hospital. Jenny's windscreen note had been intercepted by the receptionist, returning to move the car after she had seen her colleague taken away by an ambulance. Jenny was mortified – both by her own aggressive behaviour in the face of perceived adversity, and by her lack of thought that perhaps something untoward might have happened to cause the car to be left parked at such an angle. It took her quite a while to get over the emotional impact of her actions.

Jenny's weaknesses were, firstly, lack of self-management – while it was not unreasonable for her to have felt irritated by what she saw, she was unable to control the negative aspects of the way she felt, leading her to write the insulting note that she left on the other car. Secondly, Jenny lacked other-awareness. It never occurred to Jenny for one minute to question why the car might have been parked as it was – she instantly decided it was due to selfishness and thoughtlessness. Nor did she consider that the receptionist's absence might have been due to something other than her leaving work early. Her thinking was not emotionally intelligent enough to have sought for other possible reasons as to why this had happened, or to consider that it might have been caused by something other than an act of selfishness. The outcome of this lack of EI caused Jenny to feel poorly about herself, as well as having the ignominy of her colleagues not being too happy with her behaviour either.

What are emotions for?

Emotion: a moving of the feelings; agitation of the mind; any of various phenomena of the mind, such as anger, joy, fear or sorrow, associated with physical symptoms; feelings as distinguished from cognition or will.

Chambers Dictionary

There are two basic biological reasons for emotions. The first is in order to secure the survival of the species. The powerful emotions of lust, desire and love drive physical relationships between men and women and, further, the extraordinarily powerful emotion of protective love between a parent and child provides safety and protection for the child to grow and develop to adulthood.

The second reason for emotions is that they keep us safe. Without instinctive reactions to perceived danger, that have allowed humans – particularly in the early stages of humankind – to run away or prepare to fight, it is doubtful that many of us would have survived at all, especially given the scale of the threat from wild animals and inclement elements 3000 years ago. Emotions still keep us safe today. American psychiatrist Aaron Beck is famous for saying, 'Nature favours anxious genes', by which he meant that the emotions of anxiety and fear are what save us from stepping under buses or risking too much in potentially dangerous situations. It is a sad fact of life that the dare devils among us are far more likely to go to an early grave.

Emotions also affect us physiologically – especially by upping the heart rate and providing an increased blood flow to those parts of the body that need to spring into action in response to emotionally driven human action.

Imagine life without emotion

Can you imagine a life without emotions? Some of us regret falling prey to negative emotions, but without taking that risk we deny ourselves experiencing all the wonderful, positive emotions that make life so glorious and exciting for us.

Learn how our brains are involved – and how they can deceive us

To fully understand EI, it is worth learning something about its origin within our brains. We record our emotional memory in a part of the brain called the 'limbic system'. There is a small structure in the centre of the limbic system, the amygdala, and this is the centre of our emotional minds. Before any incoming data is processed by the cerebral cortex (the rational thinker), it is first vetted by the amygdala for any emotional content.

Emotion overriding rationale

The power of this emotional part of our minds to override rational intelligence, reasoned thinking and logic has been demonstrated time and time again. The amygdala specializes in emotional matters, and gives personal significance to daily events – provoking feelings of pleasure, compassion, excitement, rage and a host of other emotions.

We can look on the amygdala as a gatekeeper that scans every piece of incoming information for signs of trouble. Far quicker than the rational mind, the amygdala will take action immediately and without due regard to the consequences. If the amygdala assesses something as an emergency, it presses a 'Red Alert' button that speedily activates other parts of the brain and body.

Case study

Amy was taking a walk through the woods. When she started out on her walk, the day was sunny and bright and she was in an easy, relaxed mood. However, the weather then changed. The sun went in and dark clouds were looming. It started getting cold, a wind had sprung up, and the daylight seemed to be quickly disappearing. Suddenly, the sunny walk had turned into a chilly ordeal, and Amy decided to head for home. Just as she turned back, she heard a noise. She stopped, waited and listened. Into the silence came the sound of quiet footsteps: one or two twigs snapping and leaves crunching. Amy could see nothing. But the distant sounds crept closer to her. Her heart was now in her mouth. It was dark. Amy was alone – but not quite. Someone was there. She could feel her heart beating hard and fast. Her stomach was in knots and her legs were like jelly. The hairs on her arms seemed to stand up. Her emotions were screaming at her that she was possibly in real danger and that she needed to run away immediately. So she did. Amy ran as fast as she could, brushing past shrubs, tripping over roots, gasping for breath and feeling panic run through her.

Eventually she came out of the woods and the daylight got brighter. She could see her car parked in the distance and ran to it. Once inside, she took some deep breaths and tried to calm herself. Wondering then if she had reacted rather extremely to what might have been nothing very much, she looked back.

Walking out of the edge of the woods, looking cautiously around, was a beautiful deer. Then another walker came by with a dog, which barked at the deer, and within a second the deer was also on the run, back into the safety of the woods.

Can you identify any point in this episode when Amy's rational mind was working, or were her actions purely based on emotions – in this case, anxiety and fear? Her decision to run away was based on emotions. This was the amygdala at work. Daniel Goleman coins a good phrase for this – 'emotional hijacking'. It is what happens when our emotions respond instantaneously – either prior to rational response, or instead of it.

There is actually a good, positive reason why our brain is structured so that the amygdala is the first port of call for information processing. It is to keep us safe. While it turned out that the walk in the woods had been safe all along – it might not have been. Had the twigs been snapped by a mugger with a knife, taking time out to rationalize what the noise might have been – or even to investigate it to check it out – could have led to disastrous and perhaps fatal consequences. In this instance, the speedy, emotion-based reaction is the best one.

How does your brain control these emotions?

However, our brain must be able to control these emotions so that they don't run away with us completely, and this is done by the neocortex, which is placed just behind the forehead. While also part of the emotional brain, the neocortex is able to *control* emotions, in order to reappraise situations and to find what might be a more appropriate response.

Nonetheless, these appraisals take longer than the instant reactions of the amygdala. This is why, in Amy's case, the amygdala first got Amy to the safety of her car before her neocortex made a more controlled assessment of the situation.

While the amygdala and neocortex sound as though they make a good team, in reality, the amygdala is the stronger of the two.

Its instinctive emotional reaction can be so strong, so powerful, that it completely overrides the neocortex's attempt to make a calmer assessment of a situation. This is why we often hear people say, 'I can't think straight' when they are emotionally upset. They really *can't* think straight – the amygdala has hijacked the neocortex.

The amygdala stores past experiences that have befallen us in order to connect these experiences to what might be happening in the present. The moment the amygdala recognizes the present experience as similar to a past one, it triggers the emotions associated with that past event – it reacts to the present as if it were the past.

Our rational mind will examine evidence presented by the current situation before making a comparison and responding accordingly, but the quicker working emotional mind – not taking the time or trouble to weigh up evidence and compare and contrast the situations – will have got there first and high emotion will be flying.

This is one reason why it is futile to try and rationalize with someone who is emotionally upset. The emotions have the upper hand, and reason has flown out of the window.

Where do emotions come from?

Spend a little time thinking through your own emotions and trying to figure out where they come from. This will help you to be able to recognize emotions within yourself.

Exercise 4

What creates an emotion? If you have an answer, write it down.

I suspect you may write 'An event' or 'A circumstance' – in other words, something that has happened that produces fear, anxiety, joy, excitement and so on. In reality, it is not the event that creates the emotion, but *your thoughts* about the event. Let's go back to Amy's walk in the woods to explain this.

It might seem that the darkness in the woods coupled with the snapping of twigs and the crunching of leaves caused Amy to feel fear and panic. What actually caused those emotions was the thought behind the event – something along the lines of, 'That noise must mean someone is there and I am in danger.' Had

Amy's neocortex been able to operate without the amygdala getting in first, Amy might simply have thought, 'I wonder if that is perhaps a fox or a deer,' and, while perhaps still anxious and alert, her emotions would have been far less fraught.

Learning from childhood experiences

Childhood experiences play a huge part in our ability to develop, experience and express our emotions. When a child is brought up in a loving, emotionally open family, they will find it easy to express emotion as an adult. Unfortunately, many children grow up in malfunctioning families – where no one expresses emotions or, even worse, the child learns to block emotions. For example, a child may learn that if they cry when their elder brother teases them, they are teased even more. If their lip trembles with fear when their father urges them to ride a bike without stabilizers for the first time, they are ridiculed for being a wimp. If they get angry when they are unfairly treated, they may receive a physical punishment for expressing their resentment. So the child grows up learning to block emotions, to suppress what they feel and to live in a more emotion-free way. A child who grows up in this way will have great difficulty in becoming an emotionally open adult and may need professional help in order to change this. Psychotherapy is a good example of an enabler for the process of becoming emotionally open, with the client engaging in systematic emotional relearning. Therapy teaches people to both activate and control their emotional responses so that they can develop their emotions and use them appropriately and intelligently.

The brain as a memory store

Brains always store memories that have had a powerful effect on us emotionally, and these memories are tucked away in the amygdala. When a trigger reminds us of a past event, we will usually react in exactly the way that we did previously, even though it may be inappropriate on this occasion.

I recently worked with a client who had suffered trauma when she had been a passenger in a lift that got stuck between floors in an office block. The panic and fear she felt then resurfaced in exactly the same way every time she so much as saw a lift. In other words, her brain had stored an emotional memory that was activated any time she went near a lift – even the safe, glass-all-round, lifts that go up and down a couple of floors in shopping centres. She is fine now, after some sessions of cognitive behavioural therapy to challenge her erroneous thoughts and beliefs, but her experience serves as an excellent example of the way the brain will not always trigger the most appropriate and most helpful emotions in a new circumstance; it normally runs on past performance.

When passion overwhelms reason

Light the fire within.

Theme of the Winter Olympics, Salt Lake City, Utah, 2002

Emotions play a large part in our ability to manage both ourselves and our relationships with others. Books, plays and history itself are littered with accounts of strong emotion overruling every rational rebuttal and taking the owner of such passion towards actions that they would say were 'beyond control'. These are not instances where an emotional response is the first response – the response made before more reasoned thinking comes to the rescue. These are instances where emotional thinking positively overwhelms and outflanks any efforts that rationale might make to temper it.

This does not always mean that a response based purely on emotion will bring a negative outcome. History certainly does not show us this, and neither does psychological research. It does show that even when an emotion is so strong that it will not be brooked by reason, the outcome will be good when this strong emotion is *appropriate*.

Think of anger, one of the strongest emotions, alongside perhaps passionate love. It is also one of the most destructive and frightening of emotions when used inappropriately, but it is anger that brings about much good in the world. Often, it is only when people become so angry about a situation – poverty, starvation, a country ruled by a despot – that they fight and, if they can, correct injustice. This is anger as a high emotion used appropriately, where calm reason might not challenge the injustice strongly enough on its own, and passion is needed to motivate and activate the situation. Harnessing this highest of emotions in an emotionally intelligent way is discussed in Chapter 07.

> **Key point:** Don't make the assumption that acting on strong emotion rather than rationale is always wrong.

Your two minds

It is now fairly obvious that we have not one mind but two. Our rational mind talks common sense to us and attempts to save us from rash actions and decisions, while our emotional mind tends to colour our judgement (not only for the worse but often for the better), provides us with much positive motivation – the thrill we get from one success encouraging us to try for more – and often saves us from ourselves, for example, when anxiety tells us not to stand too close to the edge of the train platform.

Case study

David had to leave London and drive to Heathrow airport to catch a plane to Milan. In Milan he was to sign a multi-million deal contract for his company. This was the most important day in his working life, so far.

David left plenty of time to drive to the airport, park the car and check in. He factored in bad traffic, a few hold-ups and possibly needing to fill up with petrol.

What he did not factor in was a burst tyre and the fact that changing it himself brought such grief that he had to call out an automobile service to finish the job properly.

When David finally got to the airport, he ran to the check-in desk, only to be told that his flight had gone.

Exercise 5

Which comment from the airline desk clerk do you think upset David more?

a) 'I'm sorry Sir, your flight left 30 minutes ago.'
b) 'I'm sorry Sir, your flight left two minutes ago.'

When the above conundrum was tested on a variety of people, one or two said it made no difference. However, the majority of those asked leaned towards b) as the most upsetting. This is an example of the emotional mind overriding the rational mind. A plane missed is a plane missed (our rational mind tells us) – but to miss it by just two minutes is *far* more upsetting than to miss it by 30 minutes (our emotional mind tells us).

> **Key point:** Begin to have more awareness of when your emotional mind kicks in and overrules your rational mind.

The new secrets of success in life

I have touched already on the new science of positive psychology, in Chapter 01. Many of the ideas behind positive psychology incorporate the development of EI, with EI being the necessary base from which such positive personal development can ensue. The positive psychologists say, 'Let us teach you what you will need in order to reach your optimum potential.'

Positive psychology holds at its heart the ideal of teaching people the strengths and virtues that will bring them authentic and long-lasting happiness. Years of research have gone into establishing the most important of these for success, contentment and quality of life. This research has shown that universally – across 3000 years of history, across the entire face of the earth, across every mainstream religion and philosophy known to humans – six personal strengths stand out. These are:

- wisdom and knowledge
- courage
- love and humanity
- justice
- temperance
- spirituality.

EI is the engine oil of these personal strengths. It is the conductor through which such strengths and virtues can be achieved. Therefore, EI becomes the key to the door of a happy and fulfilled life.

Summary

In this chapter, we have looked at why EI is so important in order to live a life of value, success and contentment.

- You have learned a great deal more about the 'E' in emotional intelligence – where emotions come from, why we need them, and how they can deceive and distort, as well as encourage and motivate us.

- You have learned about how the emotional part of your brain works – how the amygdala jumps in very quickly and the consequent importance of gaining emotional control to achieve the best outcomes in life.
- You have learned more about the newer research into success and happiness.

The rest of this book is devoted to teaching you specific skills for developing EI in all areas of your life.

part two

two

emotional intelligence

and you: becoming

personally competent

Emotional intelligence (EI) has two main components – how we deal with ourselves (our intra-personal relationship) and how we deal with others (our inter-personal relationships). In Part two, you will learn how to understand and improve your relationship with yourself, and how to better manage your thoughts, emotions and behaviours – your intra-personal relationship. Part three will concentrate on your inter-personal relationships.

If your emotional abilities aren't in hand, if you don't have self-awareness, if you are not able to manage your distressing emotions, if you can't have empathy and have effective relationships, then no matter how smart you are, you are not going to get very far.

Daniel Goleman, psychologist and writer

03

how do you see yourself?

In this chapter you will learn:
- to identify your emotions
- to manage your emotions
- to choose your personal values.

Being emotionally intelligent means, first of all, knowing yourself. People with this competence:

- know which emotions they are feeling and why
- realize the links between their feelings and what they think, do and say
- recognize how their feelings affect their performance
- have an awareness of their values and goals.

Being able to accurately assess yourself in these areas is a vital start to making change. It is important to:

- be aware of your strengths and weaknesses
- be reflective, and be able to learn from past experiences, good and bad
- be open to honest feedback, new perspectives, continuous learning and self-development
- have a good, visible sense of humour and a sense of perspective about yourself.

Identify your own strengths and weaknesses

Here is a test that I give to many of my clients, half of which they find easy, and half of which they find very difficult. I will leave you to guess which is which.

Exercise 6

Take your watch off your wrist and set it beside you. You need to time yourself as you do this test, so don't start until you have made a note of the start time. For the first part of this test, start now.

1 List your top ten weaknesses or faults.

Stop the clock! How long did that take you? Make a note below.

Time taken 5 mins 24 sec.

Now start the clock again, and complete the second part of this test.

2 List your top ten qualities and strengths.

Stop the clock again. Record your time taken.

Time taken 3 mins 3 sec.

What have you discovered? I suspect that:

- you found the first part of the test much easier than the second part
- you may have wished for more space for the first part of the test, yet were scratching about to find ten points for the second part
- your time record will show that you took a great deal longer to complete the second part of the test than the first

What does this tell you?

- That you are a person with hundreds of faults and few good qualities?

Or

- That your view of yourself is pessimistic, and perhaps slanted towards a great deal of self-criticism? In other words, an emotionally unintelligent perception.

The second view is almost certainly going to be your real problem. However, *it actually doesn't matter whether you believe either the first or the second view*. As you will learn, an emotionally intelligent view of yourself doesn't involve considering yourself to be near perfect, but it does involve being both realistic and kind to yourself, rather than pessimistic and harsh.

All that matters is that you are comfortable with yourself – *however you are*. This means that you are looking at yourself in an emotionally intelligent way.

A tip for silencing your inner critic

Imagine that your negative views of yourself are booming out from a radio. Simply picture the radio in your mind, and then imagine yourself turning the volume down, or fiddling with the tuner button until you find another station.

Recognize the difference between your Ideal Self and your Actual Self

American psychologist Carl Rogers developed a psychological model that he called 'Person-centred'. He believed that everyone has the built-in motivation present to develop their potential to the fullest extent possible. Rogers called this our 'actualizing tendency'. His definition of an emotionally healthy person is that of an emotionally intelligent one (he used his own term, 'fully functioning', but we might well label this as being 'emotionally intelligent'). He stated that each of us has an idea of our Ideal Self – the person we would really like to be. However, most of us have views about ourselves that don't always match our Ideal Selves – and this Rogers called our Real or Actual Self. The more closely our Ideal Self and our Actual Self match, the more healthy (emotionally intelligent) we will be.

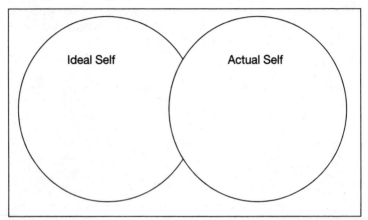

Figure 2 An emotionally unhealthy sense of self

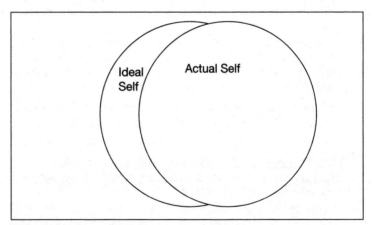

Figure 3 A healthy sense of self

The core values that equate to modern emotional intelligence

It is worth looking at Rogers' defined core values for his fully functioning, emotionally intelligent person. Developed by Rogers back in the 1960s, before EI was defined, there are similarities with Goleman's work 30 years later. Rogers suggests the following qualities will develop us intelligently:

- **Openness to experience.** This means having an accurate perception of your experiences in the world and being able to accept reality including your emotions. Rogers emphasizes that being open to your emotions is vital to personal development – his 'self-actualization', our 'emotional intelligence' (EI).   3
- **Living in the here and now.** This is the concept of accepting the past and not unduly ruminating over things that have happened and cannot be changed, or placing too much emphasis on an unknown future. It means being truly present and available within the moment, in order to experience it fully.   2
- **Trusting ourselves** to do what feels right and what comes naturally. This does not mean going out to commit murder because it 'feels right', but trusting your emotionally intelligent instincts to guide you in the right direction.   4
- **Using freedom well.** We feel free when choices are available to us. Rogers felt that the fully functioning (emotionally intelligent) person acknowledges such freedom and takes responsibility for their choices.   4
- **Being creative.** If you feel free and responsible, you will act accordingly, and participate in the world. This can be through creativity in the arts or sciences, through social concern and parental love, or simply by doing your best at your job.   2

Rogers' emphasis on identifying and being open to emotions is exactly the stuff of modern-day EI. Now test yourself.

Exercise 7

Look at the five qualities listed above and rate how strongly you believe you possess them yourself.

0 = not at all   5 = quite a lot

Hopefully, you will score reasonably throughout (25 being the highest score; 0 the lowest). If so, this means you have a good baseline EI already, and you are perhaps simply looking to increase it (or you have discovered that you already have EI in abundance and can throw this book away).

Developing your emotional self-awareness

Emotional self-awareness means giving ongoing attention to your internal state of mind, recognizing what you are feeling and why you are feeling it, and identifying events that can lead to upsets and emotional hijackings. This can mean paying attention to what you see and hear, and not to what you *think* you see and hear.

Case study

Anthony had an appointment at the osteopath, and had specifically requested it at 1.30 p.m. so that he could use his lunch break from work to attend, rather than have to ask for time off, which he was loathe to do. His job wasn't looking too secure at present, and there were redundancy rumours, so he was especially anxious not to be seen to be taking time out from his job for any reason at all. Anthony's general anxiety was compounded by worry about an elbow injury, and what it might mean, so when a friend had recommended a private osteopath, this seemed a good way to discover what was wrong without all the 'jumping through hoops' he felt he might be asked to do via the National Health Service.

Anthony arrived in good time for his appointment, but did notice that there were many other people in the waiting room. He presumed that they were also trying to squeeze this into their lunch breaks, and began to get a little nervous about the time. As 1.30 p.m. approached, Anthony became very anxious indeed, listening intently for his name to be called. Finally it was – but together with a number. 'Anthony Murphy, number 23.' Anthony was appalled. He had waited all this time, specifically requested the appointment time, and now he was being told that he was number 23 in the queue. His anger and resentment overwhelmed him. Coupled with the anxiety he had already been experiencing, he could scarcely think straight. He got up and marched out of the clinic, without so much as a by-your-leave to the receptionist, and headed back to work, his elbow still giving him lots of pain.

Finally, Anthony calmed down, but his resentment remained. So he wrote an angry letter to the clinic telling him exactly what he thought of their time-keeping. By return, he got a very polite letter, empathizing with his disappointment – but explaining that the number 23 was simply the cubicle number to which he was expected to proceed and where the osteopath was waiting for him. Enclosed with the polite letter was a bill for Anthony's non-attendance.

Anthony's story is a good example of emotional hijacking. This can come about for two reasons:

1 We misinterpret what we hear or what is actually happening. Instead of thinking things through, we jump to a conclusion that then becomes a fact in our minds. We fail to challenge this or check out its accuracy, but simply act on it.

2 We allow ourselves to become so emotionally worked up about what has happened that we lose track of rational behaviour and decision making, and instead fire off on misplaced emotions.

So how do we begin to develop the emotional self-awareness necessary to avoid such confrontations? The answer lies in personal competence. This means knowing yourself and doing the most that you can with what you have. This will give you a consistently wide choice of behaviour options, and tap in strongly to the parts of your brain that will help you out the most in particular situations.

In order to develop personal competence, you will need to learn:

• to recognize and accurately label your emotions, and to achieve this early enough to be able to control them, before they get out of hand and control you

• to give yourself choices of how to react, rather than letting it be an automatic 'I simply couldn't help it' reaction

• to become more confident in reacting appropriately, so that it becomes second nature to you

• to develop your emotional thinking so that you have a variety of flexible, appropriate ways of responding to situations.

This is not as difficult as it seems. Remember, you are reading this book in order to learn new skills, but you will not be beginning from a standing start – you will already have a great number of EI skills and abilities. You are now learning to use these to best effect – to create a better life and opportunities more easily than before.

Start by learning to recognizing your emotions

Obviously, what you don't recognize, you can't manage. If you decide that there's nothing wrong, then you won't change. However, to begin with, start thinking about emotions very specifically. We refer to ourselves and/or others as 'getting or becoming emotional'. Now you need to learn to label your emotions very accurately so that you can decide whether they are appropriate or not for a particular situation.

> **Key point:** Don't make the mistake of thinking that emotions are bad things. They are vital to us, and important enabling signals. Those with low emotion lead restricted lives with poor inter-personal communication. Here, we are aiming for appropriate emotion – emotion that guides us to good outcomes, rather than inappropriate emotion that will engender the likelihood of a bad outcome.

Exercise 8

You need to get used to identifying and labelling your emotions more specifically. Write down at least six emotions connected to each of the following:

1 happiness
2 fear
3 anger
4 depression.

A clue to get you started: happiness could involve such emotions as delight, excitement and pleasure.

You need to understand the importance of the above exercise if you are to undertake it with any enthusiasm. What do you think the importance might be? Write your answer down. Now look at the end of the chapter for the answer.

Learning to manage your emotions

Once you are used to identifying and labelling your emotions specifically, you will find it much easier to develop appropriate reactions to them. The example of 'I don't know what came over me' leaves you looking for a solution. However, 'I was overcome with apprehension' gives you valuable information – you might need to deal with what made you apprehensive so that you can handle the situation confidently next time.

> *When I say 'manage emotions' I only mean the really distressing, incapacitating emotions. Feeling emotions is what makes life rich. You need your passions.*
>
> Daniel Goleman, psychologist and writer

Exercises for managing your emotions

Now that you have begun to identify your emotions more specifically, it is time to start managing them. The next two exercises will be excellent for this, and I would suggest that you take several photocopies of the questionnaires and use them on a regular basis. To begin with, try to go through each of them two or three times a week. Review your learning after a month and decide whether to do the same for a further month, or reduce the activity to once a week for the next month. Again, review your learning at the end of that month, and plan to either increase or decrease the time you spend on this, according to your assessment of your abilities.

Exercise 9

- Describe a situation during the last month in which you successfully identified and managed your own emotions and those of others.
- What emotions did you identify in yourself and the other person or people?
- What skills did you use to manage your emotions?
- What skills did you use to manage the emotions of the other person or people?

Exercise 10

- Describe a situation in the last month where you felt you were unsuccessful in correctly identifying your own emotions, and possibly those of others as well.
- What emotions did you have difficulty identifying in yourself and in the other person or people?
- What skills would you like to have had (you may be able to identify these from looking at examples you have given in Exercise 9) so that you could have managed your emotions more effectively?
- What steps can you now take to develop these skills?
- Can you identify any costs and/or benefits to taking these steps?

Learn to become more open about your emotions

Being willing to tell others how we feel is extremely self-empowering. It helps others to understand our thoughts and actions, and this in turn has the effect of increasing our own confidence in what we are feeling, saying and doing.

The Johari Window

You may already be familiar with the Johari Window; however, it is such an important concept in relation to openness that I refer to it here. If you are an expert already, move on! Incidentally, while its name sounds exotic and meaningful, it is nothing more than a fusion of the Christian names of the two people who thought it up – Joseph Luft and Harry Ingham.

	Known to self	Not known to self
Known to others	1 OPEN	2 BLIND
Not known to others	3 HIDDEN	4 UNKNOWN

Figure 4 The Johari Window

The Johari Window is a useful model to describe how we relate to others. A four-paned 'window', as illustrated in Figure 4, divides personal awareness into four different types represented by its four quadrants: open, hidden, blind and unknown.

In this model, each person is represented by their own window. First, imagine mine:

1 The open quadrant represents things that you and I both know about me (for example, I know my name, and so do you). The knowledge that the window represents can include not only factual information but also my feelings, motives, behaviours, wants, needs and desires – indeed, any information describing who I am that I am willing to divulge to you. The more that I am willing to tell you about myself, the better you will get to know and understand me, and the better I learn to know myself, based on my openness and your listening and possible input.

2 The blind quadrant represents things that you know about me, but that I am unaware of. So, for example, we could be eating at a restaurant, and I may have unknowingly got some spinach stuck in my teeth. This information is in my blind quadrant because you can see it, but I cannot. Of course, if you tell me about the spinach, the transaction moves to the open quadrant.

More importantly, I may have blind spots about my emotions. For instance, during our conversation, you may notice that eye contact seems to be lacking. You may not say anything, since you do not want to embarrass me, or you may draw your own inferences that perhaps I am feeling insincere or embarrassed about something. The problem then becomes mine: how can I get this information out in the open since it may be affecting the level of trust that is developing between us? How can I learn more about myself? The answers, of course, are that I need to work out for myself the emotion(s) I am feeling, and be willing to share these with you, so that we both understand what is going on for me.

3 The hidden quadrant represents things that I know about myself but that you do not know. In the case of my emotions, for example, I am feeling insecure just now because I have been told that I may lose my job – but I don't want to discuss this with you as I feel so embarrassed about it. This information is in my hidden quadrant. As soon as I am willing to tell you my concerns, and describe to you how I feel, I am effectively moving the information in my hidden quadrant to the open quadrant's area. This is the self-disclosure that is so helpful to us in developing self-awareness. Once we have placed something about ourselves 'out in the open', we are often more willing to accept it as a truth, rather than hide or deny it.

4 The unknown quadrant represents things that neither I know about myself, nor you know about me. This probably sounds a little strange! However, imagine, for instance, that I am usually quite a cowardly, self-interested type of person, yet walking along the street with you one day we see an elderly lady being mugged. I immediately rush up to help, beat off the attacker and assist the older lady to her feet. Both you and I are staggered that I have done this. I didn't know I had it in me, and you certainly would not have imagined that I had it in me. Between us, we have discovered that I possess more positive emotions than I had thought – anger at unprovoked bad treatment, sympathy for someone hurt, courage in adversity. Moreover, the negative emotions I had assumed would rise to the fore – fear, cowardice, even lack of interest in a stranger's situation – had been wrongly identified. Thus, a novel situation can trigger new awareness and personal growth.

Using the Johari Window model to improve self disclosure

Much more has been written on the Johari Window model of human interaction than our brief look at it here. The process of enlarging the open quadrant is called 'self-disclosure', a give-and-take process between you and the people you interact with. Typically, as you share something about yourself (moving information from your hidden quadrant into the open one), the person you are talking to will reciprocate, by similarly disclosing information in their hidden quadrant. Thus, an interaction between two people can be modelled dynamically as two active Johari Windows. For example, you may respond to my disclosure that I am concerned about my job with information that your own company is looking for personnel with exactly my qualifications.

Remember, the blind quadrant contains behaviour, feelings and motivations not accessible to the person, but which others can see. Feelings of inadequacy, incompetence, unworthiness, rejection, guilt and a need to control and manipulate are all difficult to face and yet can be seen by others.

As a person's level of confidence and self-esteem develops, he or she may actively invite others to comment on their blind spots. A teacher may seek feedback from students on the quality of a particular lecture, with the desire of improving the presentation. Active listening skills are helpful in this endeavour.

This is one of the most important reasons to develop strong self-awareness. Being unable to see ourselves as others see us is hugely limiting, and results in a failure to control our lives and in others making life choices on our behalf that may be far from what we want or hope for.

Where your interaction with others is not congruent, genuine and open – for example, perhaps you always put on a smiling, happy face, and hide all negative feelings – you may be signalling to your friends or colleagues to withhold as well, and to keep their distance. Thus, your communication style may seem bland or distant.

Before moving away from self-disclosure, a word about appropriateness. This can sometimes be a grey area, and we discover too late that we have shared too much. By self-disclosure, we are not talking about going overboard and telling everyone everything! You will have the intelligence, in general terms, to know what is appropriate and inappropriate. However, since I am encouraging you to test the waters of personal disclosure as a way of increased self-awareness, I need to alert you to the importance of appropriateness.

Exercise 11

To help you become more open with self-disclosure, disclose a small piece of information to see what reaction you get. You can then adjust your level of personal disclosure to embrace this.

Self-awareness in relation to others

Your self-awareness needs to extend to being aware of other's reactions to your behaviour.

Case study

Peter and Bill were shopping for a suitcase for Bill to take on holiday. When they entered the luggage department, they were greeted by an attractive sales assistant, who smiled and asked if she could help. 'Well, my love life's a little flat right now,' said Pete. 'Could you help with that?' Bill blushed and quickly intercepted, 'I'm looking for a strong suitcase.' 'No problem,' said the sales girl. 'What size are you looking for?' Before Bill could reply, Peter chipped in with, 'Well, one that you could fit into as well would be good.' Bill turned to Peter. 'Will you shut up? All I wanted to do was buy a suitcase, not listen to you embarrassing yourself with someone young enough to be your daughter. I'll go and buy my own suitcase.' Apologizing to the salesgirl, Bill walked off, with Peter calling after him, 'Keep your hair on. What's eating you today?'

Peter's capacity for self-awareness was almost non-existent. He had no idea of the negative effect his behaviour was having on both the salesgirl and his friend. He was oblivious to the fact that he was looking like an idiot, or that he might be causing embarrassment to others.

Key point: Becoming aware of how others may feel about your behaviour gives you an opportunity to change your actions. If someone reacts in an unexpected or disappointing way, never think 'Oh, it's just them'. Look at your own style of speech and behaviour and work on the possibility that this may need adjusting to achieve a better result. Keep in mind the saying, 'It's not what you say that matters, it's what others actually hear.'

Exercise 12

To help you increase your self-awareness, keep a brief daily diary over the next week. In it, write down the following:

- The strongest emotion you felt on that day.
- The circumstances in which you felt it.
- How this emotion made you react.
- Was your reaction appropriate?
- If anyone else was present, how did they interpret your response? (If you were alone, ask yourself this question hypothetically.)
- Now ask yourself – are you sure that the other person would have seen things the way you think they would?

As always, your interest in carrying out the above exercise will depend on your appreciating its purpose. What do you think its purpose is? Write your answer down.

The explanation is that by keeping this diary you are learning to develop self-awareness regarding your behaviour in relation to others. Most of us use this skill far too rarely. We tend to 'shoot from the hip', 'say how we feel', 'run with our emotions' – and fail to have enough EI to work out that we may not be behaving appropriately. This is all part of learning to manage yourself.

Be honest with yourself

When we looked at the Johari Window, I discussed being open with others. Being open with yourself is just as important. You are the one person you cannot fool. This does not mean beating yourself up and giving yourself a hard time. It means using balanced and rational reflection, monitoring your feelings, and checking on their appropriateness to situations – then being willing to admit to yourself that perhaps you could have done better or differently, and to learn from that experience.

In life, there is no such thing as failure. There are successes, and there are learning experiences.

Petruschka Clarkeson, psychology professor

Develop the confidence to appreciate this wise saying. When you get something wrong, you are not failing if you are learning from it. Even Peter from the case study above, who so embarrassed his friend Bill and the shop assistant, might have salvaged something from the experience if it led to him 'replaying the video' and looking at acting differently when placed in a similar situation in future. Be emotionally intelligent with yourself.

Choosing your personal values

Exercise 13

What values do you believe are important for emotionally intelligent living? You may consider that you have some of these values already, or that you believe they are worth developing. Write six down now.

As mentioned in Chapter 02, positive psychology has attempted to identify core values – such as those listed on p. 35 – which stand out as virtues most likely to provide a happy and contented life on an enduring basis. The values identified are developed by and incorporated into emotionally intelligent living.

Stephen Covey, author of *The Seven Habits of Highly Effective People*, has made a study of the core values he believes will take people forward to happiness and success both personally and professionally.

Here is a list of values that these two studies consider to be among the most important. Take a look and compare them to your answers to Exercise 13.

*Wisdom and knowledge	*Courage	*Love and humanity
*Justice	*Temperance	*Spirituality
Responsibility	Humility	Vision
Kindness	Gratitude	Forgiveness
Social intelligence	Perspective	Integrity
Humour	Motivation	Fairness
Self-control	Prudence	Humility

*Denotes positive psychology's six basic virtues, found by research to be constant over 'Three thousand years and the entire face of the earth' (Seligman, 2003, p.132).

These qualities are all defined as emotionally intelligent virtues. Developing your EI will encourage these qualities within you. Equally, developing at least some of these individual qualities will ensure that your EI develops as a default. Positive psychology argues that there is a direct relationship between possessing these core values and developing EI.

Self-esteem

William James (1890) defined self-esteem as: 'The feeling of self-worth that derives from the ratio of our actual successes to our pretensions [hopes] for success.' This definition of self-esteem highlights the idea that it addresses the way we evaluate ourselves and measure our own sense of self-worth by comparing how we are and how we aspire to be. (In this regard, it is similar to Carl Rogers' Ideal Self and Actual Self theory discussed earlier.)

What is the difference between self-esteem and self-confidence?

Self-confidence is a result of self-esteem. It is self-esteem in action. If we feel good, we will try more, stretch ourselves more and believe that we can – we are confident enough in our abilities to do so. Self-confident people will:

- present themselves with self-assurance and have 'presence'
- voice views that are unpopular and go out on a limb for what is right
- be decisive and be able to make sound decisions despite uncertainties and pressures.

Self-confidence is the keeper of our actions and reactions. Without it, we can find ourselves acting in a way that we – either at the time or later – regret. We may find ourselves tongue-tied at a time when we wish to speak eloquently. We may react angrily or defensively when we need to be calm and assertive. We may say too much, say too little, stay when we should go, go when we should stay, and so on. Unless your self-confidence is rock solid and never fails you, you will be familiar with some of these situations. Self-esteem is about *being*. Self-confidence is about *doing*.

There is a myriad of reasons for the onset and development of poor self-confidence. While it is not within the remit of this book to dwell unduly on these, in general many of these reasons can come from childhood criticisms or dysfunctional beliefs that we bring with us into adulthood. Sometimes our confidence is knocked in later life, for example, by the breakdown of a significant relationship, job loss, bereavement or ill health. Any of these things can cause us to lose resilience and feel defeated and unhappy.

The problem is that lack of confidence can be a self-fulfilling prophecy. We don't believe that we can succeed so we don't try. Not trying increases our belief that we are incapable. We can become completely stuck and feel that we have no ability to change our uselessness and lack of ability.

In Chapter 04, we take a look at the enormous power of our thoughts in defining what we do, fail to do, achieve and fail to achieve. You will learn that by changing your thinking, you can change how you feel. You can replace unproductive thinking with emotionally intelligent thinking – and it really will change your life.

Summary

In this chapter we have looked at and assessed your levels of self-awareness – an important component of EI.

- The core premise of EI is that you must 'know yourself' before you can become emotionally intelligent. This is why you were asked to list what you perceive to be your strengths and weaknesses in Exercise 6. Hopefully this made you think about yourself in a little more depth.

- Identifying your emotions in a more specific way than you have perhaps been used to is extremely important. Without such identification, it is impossible to understand exactly what is going on, and how you can effectively make productive changes.

- Managing emotions is not easy. Until faced with the fact that it is possible to do so (I assure you of this now), many people believe that they must just run with their emotions, and have no control over them, i.e. their emotions control them, and thus control outcomes and results.

- We do have control over our emotions, but it is hard at first and takes practice.

- Regularly do the exercises in this chapter in order to achieve control over your emotions.

- Becoming more open about our emotions can be hard for some people, although it has enormous benefits for self-development and self-knowledge. Look again at the Johari Window. The idea behind it – to move as much as we can to the open window – is a worthwhile aim.

- An increased awareness of how our words and deeds affect others is an important skill. People who perform well in this area are usually regarded as having great personal charm or charisma. When we are with such people, we feel attended to and listened to, very 'present' with that person. Work hard to develop this attribute and your social skills (and popularity) will increase enormously.

The relationship between the identified core values that constitute the ingredients for a full and happy life and EI is now well documented. Hopefully, this also gives you something more to work towards. The blueprint is there, all 'checked and correct' – just follow it.

Assessing your levels of esteem and confidence and then – unless they are already extremely high – working on these is vital for good EI. They go hand in hand. Working on developing these values – which you can do with the confidence of knowing that their validity has been researched and proven – will increase your EI. Equally, good EI will make it easier for you to build these values into your life.

Answer: Having a broader choice of emotions to choose from in any given situation will help you to become far more accurate in defining your feelings. Start to discard expressions such as 'I felt awful' or 'I don't know what came over me' and begin to replace them with more accurate definitions like 'I felt filled with remorse' or 'I was overcome with apprehension'. In other words, you will start recognizing your emotions.

04

thinking straight

In this chapter you will learn:
- the value of positive thinking
- how your thinking style affects your emotions
- how to identify and challenge negative thoughts
- that it is not what happens to you, but your perceptions of what has happened that decides your reactions.

The power of positive thinking

Positive thinking engenders positive emotions. Both Daniel Goleman and Martin Seligman stress the importance of the way we think in both managing negative emotions and in creating positive emotions.

Goleman cites people who are prone to worry when asked to perform a task as usually performing very poorly. They think along the lines of 'I won't be able to do this' or 'I'm just no good at this kind of thing'. However, these people, on being taught various skills to enhance their negative thinking – such as relaxation (to reduce the body's response to anxiety), humour (good moods tend to enhance our ability to think more flexibly), thought challenging (cognitive therapy that encourages us to re-evaluate the validity of our negative thinking and replace these thoughts with more balanced and positive ones) were able to easily return to the tasks at a later stage and perform them very well.

Seligman also points out that how you think about your problems will affect your emotions either positively or negatively. He suggests that some of us lean naturally towards a pessimistic explanatory style that encourages negative emotions and precludes too many glimpses of positive ones.

Let's look at how using these various skills can help you.

Using relaxation

Many people think that learning to relax means lying on a mat in a quiet place and playing a CD of soothing music to calm you down, perhaps sea sounds or jungle noises. While not invalidating this method of relaxation, when emotions are running high you will need a relaxation skill that will work quickly and will work anywhere. Muscular relaxation is ideal for this.

Exercises to help you relax quickly and easily

Try the following exercises every day for a week. At the end of the week, pick the four you like best (i.e. whichever make you feel the most relaxed), and practise them each day for three days. Then select your two preferred exercises from the four and for two days simply try those two. At the end of this period, choose the one exercise that helps you to relax most successfully and most quickly. Simply keep this in the back of your mind and whenever you feel worrying thoughts and negative emotions beginning to start up, use this relaxation exercise (possibly several times over) until you feel calmer.

- Clench your fists. Hold for 10 seconds and then release for about 15–20 seconds.
- Tighten your biceps muscles by drawing your forearms up towards your shoulders and 'making a muscle' with both arms. Hold for about 10 seconds and then relax for 15–20 seconds.
- Tighten your forehead muscles by raising your eyebrows as high as you can. Hold for about 10 seconds, and then relax for 15–20 seconds.
- Tighten up the muscles around your eyes by clenching your eyes tightly shut. Hold for about 10 seconds and then relax for 15–20 seconds.
- Tighten the muscles in the back of your neck by gently leaning your head way back, as if you were going to touch your head to your back. Focus only on tensing the muscles in your neck. Hold for about 10 seconds and then relax for 15–20 seconds. Repeat this step if your neck muscles feel especially tight.
- Tighten your shoulders by raising them up as if you were going to touch your ears with them. Hold for about 10 seconds and then relax for 15–20 seconds.
- Tighten the muscles around your shoulder blades by pushing your shoulder blades back as if you were trying to push them together. Hold the tension in your shoulder blades for about 10 seconds, and then relax for 15–20 seconds. Repeat this step if your upper back feels especially tight.

Using deep breathing

When you suffer from negative emotions, your breathing tends to be tight and shallow. You breathe from your chest rather than your abdomen and fail to oxygenate your body properly.

Practise deep breathing at home on a regular basis (don't leave this until your emotions wind you up or you won't get enough practice). Sit in a comfortable chair and become really aware of your breathing. Focus on taking deeper breaths and slowing your breathing down. Think about the pre-sleep breathing that flows naturally before you drift off, and look to achieve a similar state.

Using humour

Goleman cites the intellectual benefits of 'a good laugh'. Telling or listening to jokes, watching a humorous television programme, and spending time with humorous people have all been shown to enhance our cognitive (thinking) skills and make it easier for us to feel optimistic and motivated.

One simple way of introducing humour into your frame of mind can be to recall a few anecdotal memories of funny moments in your own life. We all have them, and focusing on a few so that they can be more easily recalled from your memory when you need them can be a useful source of relaxation and calming negative emotions.

Using cognitive challenging

Relaxation and humour will work 'in the moment'. But for more permanent solutions to the problems of becoming held in the thrall of inappropriate emotions, cognitive work will serve you well. Our emotions always stem from the thoughts we have. So to manage our emotions, we need to become emotionally intelligent thinkers.

In the rest of this chapter, you will learn exactly how to do this. EI, fairly obviously, requires thinking intelligence. Understanding our thinking styles and how we can easily challenge them and change them is an important part of developing EI.

In order to become more intelligent emotionally, therefore, we must also learn to understand the role our thinking styles play in this.

Learning the skills for thought challenging

Thinking types

Our thoughts usually fall into one of four categories:

- positive (where we always see the bright side, true or not)
- evaluative (where we give rational consideration to the options)
- neutral (thoughts that are insignificant, such as what to watch on TV, for example)
- negative (where we see the downside of something and take the bleakest view of a good outcome).

Further, our thoughts, other than the neutral ones, will tend to fall into two further sub-categories:

- self-oriented thoughts (where we spend a great deal of time worrying about outcomes in relation to ourselves)
- action-orientated thoughts (where we decide what we can do about a difficulty that might make a positive difference).

Removing neutral thoughts from the equation, it will be fairly clear that the most productive thoughts to focus on in developing an emotionally intelligent outlook are going to be:

- evaluative thoughts
- action-orientated thoughts.

Understanding that what you think manages your emotions

The way you think has an important effect on the way you feel and what you are able to do. Pessimistic, negative thoughts such as 'I can't cope' or 'I feel terrible' make you feel anxious and unhappy. Some of your thoughts may be based on reality, but some will probably be 'guesswork', and you may be jumping to conclusions that paint things blacker than they are. We call these 'negative automatic thoughts' because they are unrealistically pessimistic and because they seem to come from nowhere and 'automatically' enter your mind. You need to counter this by developing emotionally intelligent thought processes.

Learn to identify negative thoughts

Becoming aware of negative thoughts can help you to understand why you feel the way you do emotionally, and this is the first step towards learning to think in a more helpful, positive way.

To help you become more aware of these thoughts, you first need to know a little more about what negative thoughts 'look like'. The following is a list of characteristics that these thoughts have in common.

- They spring to mind without any effort from you.
- They are easy to believe.
- They are often not true.
- They can be difficult to stop.
- They are unhelpful.
- They keep you anxious and make it difficult to change.

These negative thoughts may be difficult to spot to start with – you are probably not aware that you have them – and the first step is to learn to recognize them.

You can recognize negative thoughts using a 'Thought record'. The more you practise writing down your thoughts, the easier it becomes to spot them, and to understand the effect they have on your emotions. Don't worry if you find this difficult at first. It may be quite a new idea to try to remember what you were thinking when you were worried or feeling low, and it may take some practice before you get the hang of it. Next time you find yourself becoming emotional in any way, as soon as you can, sit down and write down your accompanying thoughts. Describe the physical sensations you experienced and the thoughts that went through your head at the time.

> **Key point:** The way we think changes the way we feel. Never make the mistake of thinking that your emotions pop out of nowhere. Emotions are generated by thoughts – and we always have an opportunity to re-evaluate our thoughts to get a more positive emotional outcome.

What to do when your thoughts aren't clear

Sometimes, it is very difficult for us to access our worrying thoughts, and you may possibly feel that you simply don't know what was in your mind – or you might even feel certain that there was nothing in your mind – it was simply an emotion, sitting there on its own. Don't worry about this, with practice you will gradually learn to access difficult thoughts, and you can also ask yourself some simple questions to assist you. For example, 'What was I afraid might be going to happen?', 'What was happening, or what was in my mind just before I began feeling this way?' or 'Am I recalling any past incidences where things turned out poorly?'

> **Exercise 14**
>
> To help you identify your emotion-provoking thoughts, take a sheet of paper, or workbook, and rule three vertical columns, headed as in the example on the next page. Write down three events in the last week that have caused some sort of negative emotion – identify it specifically – and then write down the thought you had that generated that emotion.

Event	Emotion (rate how strongly you feel it 0–100%)	Thought (rate how strongly you believe it 0–100%)
e.g. Getting stood up for a date.	depression (70%) or anger (90%) or acceptance (100%)	'I'm unlovable.' (65%) 'How dare he/she?' (80%) 'He/she probably forgot.' (100%)

A suggestion to help you differentiate between thoughts and emotions

Thoughts tend to be sentences, even if they begin with, 'I feel...' For example, 'I feel he has treated me unfairly.' This is a thought not a feeling. Emotions tend to be single words – happy, sad, cheerful, depressed, anxious, worried, delighted, etc. The sentence above, while expressing how its owner feels about a situation, doesn't give the emotion. Think about what the emotion might be. Anger, frustration or helplessness perhaps (all one-word emotions)?

Is this the thought that has triggered my emotion?

Ensure that your thought(s) and feeling(s) 'match' by rating the thought and the emotion. For example, if your mood rating is 'panic (90%)', a negative thought on the lines of 'My friend has forgotten our lunch appointment' is not going to be the emotion-provoking thought. So ask yourself, 'Why does that matter?' and you are more likely to get to the correct causal thought – which in this case, could be 'Perhaps she has been involved in a serious accident.'

The downward arrow technique

This is another excellent skill to help you identify the thought causing your emotions. You can use it in a variety of situations – and with others as well as yourself. It works like this...

You feel dreadfully stressed and your head is aching. Why is this? Your first thought is:

'I can't seem to get on with the work I need to do for this presentation.'

The first question is: (downward arrow)

'Why does that matter?'

The answer is:

'If the presentation doesn't go well, we may lose the client.'

The second question is: (downward arrow)

'Why does that matter?'

The answer is:

'If we lose the client our department won't meet its sales targets.'

The third question is: (downward arrow)

'Why does that matter?'

The answer is:

'I'll be held responsible and I may even lose my job.'

We won't go further with 'Why does that matter?' as you will understand the principle now, but in theory of course you can ask yourself another question instead:

What is the personal meaning to me if this does or doesn't occur?

It is not always easy to ascribe emotions to our thoughts. Here are some suggestions to help you:

Am I ...?

anxious	scared	shy	panicky
insecure	sad	hurt	depressed
disappointed	empty	angry	irritated
frustrated	appalled	embarrassed	humiliated
repulsed	sick	nauseous	guilty
ashamed	jealous	envious	shocked
surprised	happy	excited	content
proud			

And there are many more emotions. You can add your own for future reference.

Understanding how your perceptions shape your thoughts

Most people tend to believe that the events in their lives cause them to feel the way they do, i.e. what actually happens is what decides the emotional response. For example, you meet a friend for a drink one evening:

You: Hello, Pete, how are things?

Pete: I feel absolutely dreadful, really bad.

You: Goodness, Pete – whatever has happened to make you feel this way?

Pete: My boss had me in his office this morning to tell me that the report I put together for our biggest client wasn't remotely up to scratch. He was extremely rude and threatened to take me off the account.

Exercise 15

To help you identify emotions specifically, firstly, let's look at Pete's emotional barometer. It's pretty high, but what exactly are his emotions? Feeling 'dreadful', feeling 'bad'. What does this mean?

You can use what you have learned about identifying emotions *specifically* to see that Pete isn't quite giving the helpful information that he could. Take a guess at what emotions might more closely identify with Pete's tale of woe. This specific identification is really important – you will see why in a moment.

Next, what is it that has made Pete feel this way? Is it:

- the fact that Pete's boss has really laid into him?

Or:

- the meaning that Pete has given to what has happened, i.e. his thoughts about the event and the personal interpretation he has given it?

If Pete's interpretation of the event was that his boss thought he was a useless idiot and Pete agreed with him, then Pete's emotions might be fear ('I'll get the sack or demoted.') or hopelessness ('I'm useless. I'll never get anywhere in life.').

If Pete's interpretation of the event was that his boss was being totally unreasonable and exaggerating the poor quality of his work, then Pete's emotions might have been anger ('How dare he speak to me like that?') or frustration ('He never gives me the smallest credit – he always finds a flaw somewhere.').

If Pete's interpretation of the event was that his work hadn't actually been quite as good as usual and that his boss was a bit of a tyrant generally, with rarely a good word to say to people, his emotions might have been reasonably calm ('He's right, my work wasn't that good this time so I need to try harder.' or 'He shouts at everyone on Monday mornings, it's not personal to me.').

In other words, one situation has a variety of possible interpretations and – most importantly – a wide variety of emotional responses.

It is not what happens to us in life that decides how we feel emotionally; the meaning we give to these events decides this.

Learn to challenge negative thoughts

Once you are familiar with identifying negative thoughts and emotions, you can keep track of them and examine how unrealistic or unhelpful they are and whether they are useful to you. If they are unrealistic or unhelpful, you can challenge them with what we call a 'balanced response' (we might also call this an emotionally intelligent response). This is a reply that you can make to these thoughts, based on firm evidence. Studies have shown that doing this can improve your mood and make you feel more in control of your situation and your life.

When you suspect that your thoughts are negative or emotionally upsetting, ask yourself:

* Is this *really* true?
* Is there another way of looking at this?

Write the answers down in your 'Thought record':

Event	Emotion (rate how strongly you feel it 0–100%)	Thought (rate how strongly you believe it 0–100%)	Is there another way of looking at this?
e.g. Getting stood up for a date.	depression (70%) or	'I'm unlovable.' (65%)	'I'm still a great person. They are the idiot.'
	anger (90%) or	'How dare he/she?' (80%)	'It's his/her loss, more than mine.'
	acceptance (100%)	'He/she probably forgot.' (100%)	'It's possible something has happened to them.'

You should by now have a better idea of how answering your negative thoughts in a more helpful, realistic way can help you to cope with your emotions. However, it can still be hard to think of positive, coping thoughts that will help you deal with your emotions. Here is a list of coping statements that may give you some ideas. Read through the list and think about which of these might apply to you and help you to deal with your emotions in a more positive and constructive way.

Examples of coping statements you might use

- I'm going to face this problem situation so that I can practise coping better.
- It's unlikely that it will work completely, but the important thing is to practise and build up my confidence.
- I know that worry makes me feel worse. I know my feelings can be controlled.
- I've been in this position before and have come out of it alive/still in one piece.
- I know I'll get better the more I get used to coping with worry.
- I'll feel so proud of myself when I feel myself getting calmer.
- It feels good learning how to control worrying feelings.
- I'm deliberately going to change how I feel.

The key to being able to think in a more balanced way is to keep practising. Every time you become aware of negative thoughts going through your mind, try to stop yourself and think of a positive, realistic answer to them.

When preparing to go into a situation that makes you anxious or worried, think about what coping skills you will use (for example, a breathing exercise) and how you will answer any negative thoughts before, during and afterwards. Being prepared is half the battle of helping you to cope.

Understand your different thinking styles

It is also important to check the *validity* of your thoughts. Often, we think we are looking at something sensibly, when in fact we are not. We tend to assume that all our thinking is rational and correct. Much of it is, of course, but we can fail to see that a great deal of it is skewed or biased and this, of course, will have a huge effect on our emotions.

Exercise 16

To help you identify different thinking styles, look at the distorted thinking styles listed below. Make a note of any that you think you might be occasionally guilty of. Don't be aghast if you note down most of them (most of us are also guilty if we're being honest!).

Styles of distorted thinking

1 Filtering

We take negative details from a situation and then 'magnify' them, while at the same time filtering out all the positive aspects. For example, you get a wine stain on your dress at a party, and it becomes all you can think about. You fail to notice the pleasant atmosphere, people having fun and enjoying the evening.

2 Polarized thinking

We decide that things are 'black or white', 'good or bad'. 'I must be perfect or I am a failure.' There is no middle ground. For example, if you fail to get an A grade in your exam, you feel terribly depressed at your stupidity rather than pleased that you did get a B grade.

3 Over-generalization

We come to a general conclusion based on a single incident or piece of evidence. If something bad happens once, we expect it to happen over and over again. If you have a car accident, you may decide to stop driving on motorways, as they are obviously dangerous places and (in your view) you are likely to have another accident the next time you go on one.

4 Mind reading

Without their saying so, we 'know' what people are thinking and why they act the way they do. In particular, we are able to divine how people are feeling towards us. How often do we hear someone say 'I know they are thinking that I'm ... (stupid/boring/unattractive/out of place, etc.)'? Believe me, if you can really read people's minds, you should be applying for a job with the intelligence service – they would be most interested in you!

5 Catastrophizing

We expect disaster. We notice or hear about a problem, and start on, 'What ifs'. 'What if tragedy strikes?' 'What if it happens to you?' Often, when we do this, we also overestimate the 'awfulness' if this thing were to happen, so that not only do we worry about an unlikely tragedy, but decide that if it did happen, it would be unbearable.

6 Personalization

We think that everything people do or say is some kind of reaction to us. We also compare ourselves to others, trying to determine who's smarter, better looking, etc. If someone says that they aren't a fan of Madonna, you assume that, since you recently went to one of her concerts, they are criticizing your taste in music (rather than expressing a personal preference).

7 Control fallacies

If we feel externally controlled, we see ourselves as helpless, as victims of fate, but this is a control fallacy. The fallacy of internal control is that you feel responsible for the pain and happiness of everyone around you. It's either 'not my fault' or 'all my fault'.

8 Fallacy of fairness

We feel resentful because we think we know what's fair, but other people won't agree with us. This can be a sign of rigid thinking – 'I'm right, so why won't you agree?'

9 Blaming

We hold other people responsible for our pain, or take the other tack and blame ourselves for every problem or reversal. This is a 'victim' mentality, and leaves us feeling we have no power or responsibility and can therefore do nothing to make a change.

10 'Shoulds'

We have a long list of 'iron-clad' rules about how we, and other people, should act. People who break our rules anger us, and we feel guilty if we break our own rules. We can become extremely upset by others' behaviour when it goes against what we believe is the 'right' way to do something. We can even get into arguments with people or terminate friendships if we feel others are not acting according to our own rules for living.

11 Emotional reasoning

We believe that what we feel must be true. If we feel stupid and boring, then we must be stupid and boring. We don't check the facts; we just run with our emotions and let them decide things for us.

12 Fallacy of change

We expect other people to change to suit us if we just pressure or cajole them enough. We try to change people in this way when we believe our hopes for happiness seem to depend entirely on their behaving differently. This is another type of 'playing the victim'. For everything to be 'all right' we need to ensure that others do what we need them to – and get very upset if they don't.

13 Globalizing

We generalize one or two negative opinions into a negative global judgement. Someone, for example, can take a view on the entire population of a particular country based on his bad experiences with one or two people who live there.

14 'Being right'

We continually put ourselves on trial to prove that our opinions and actions are correct. Being wrong is unthinkable and we will go to any lengths to demonstrate our 'rightness'. The phrase 'Being right is more important than being happy' for some people speaks for itself. Even though they are losing friends left, right and centre, some people continue to pursue a point of view to the death in an effort to prove themselves right.

15 'Heaven's reward' fallacy

We expect all our sacrifice and denial to pay off, as if someone is keeping the score. We then feel bitter when we are not recognized and rewarded for the sacrifices we have made. Otherwise known as 'martyrdom', this is very much the old 'after all I've done for you' style of thinking. It deprives those who think this way of the pleasure that comes from doing a kind thing because they are always looking to receive, and measure, pay-back.

Source: Adapted from *Thoughts and Feelings: the Art of Cognitive Stress Intervention*, McKay, Davis and Fanning (1981)

Are faulty beliefs holding you back?

You need to identify what blocks your attempts at emotionally intelligent thinking.

Understanding beliefs

We can divide our thought processes into three categories.

1 Automatic thoughts. These are the thoughts that simply pop into our heads at any given time and are usually event-specific and will generate some sort of emotion, depending on what we are thinking. For example, when you get home from work and find the door unlocked you might think, 'It's a burglar' (anxiety), 'Perhaps I forgot to lock it this morning' (annoyance with yourself) or 'Perhaps my partner has come home early for once' (happiness, hopefully!). Automatic thoughts can be positive, negative or neutral. We have been looking at automatic thoughts already in this chapter and they are, in essence, the 'top layer' of our thinking.

2 Beliefs are the 'bottom layer' of our thinking. We regard them as absolute – they are not open to debate as they are simply, in our minds, facts. We have negative beliefs about:

- ourselves ('I am worthless/brilliant.')
- others ('People always let you down./Most people are nice.')
- the world ('The country is a safe place./Crime is everywhere.')
- the future. ('Nothing stays the same./Nothing will ever change.').

Beliefs can be so deep that we rarely even consider them. We see them as absolute truths, 'just the way things are' – but they are very often wrong. They usually stem from childhood, when we rarely, if ever, question what we learn.

Case study

Anne's parents loved her very dearly, but they decided that telling her that whatever she achieved she could do even better would have a positive effect. However well Anne did, instead of being praised, she was told to 'try even harder next time'. If she got 80 per cent in a test, that was a failure and she must get 90 per cent next time. If she got 90 per cent then only 100 per cent was good enough. Not surprisingly, Anne developed a negative belief about herself along the lines of 'No matter how hard I try, I'm just not good enough.'

Anne did get herself a good job. However, she was never able to fulfil her potential, since every time she started on a piece of challenging work, her 'I'm just not good enough' belief kicked in and she would think, 'I won't be able to do a good job. I'll get it wrong and everyone will see how incompetent I am. I'll let someone else take it on, and stick to simple tasks I can't mess up.'

Telling Anne to think more positively and believe she will do a good job won't help her at all because it flies in the face of her basic belief that she isn't good enough.

In such situations, we need to learn to identify unhelpful beliefs that prevent us from thinking more openly about ourselves and life in general, and then to replace them with beliefs that are more helpful to us.

Key point: We are less aware of our negative beliefs than we are of our negative thinking. This is because we convince ourselves that our beliefs are 'truths'. Constantly remind yourself that negative beliefs are no more than a point of view that may not be true.

Exercise 17

To help you identify some of your beliefs, consider any strong beliefs you might have about yourself. Write them down. Ask yourself, at this moment, how strongly you believe each of them using a scale of 1 = not much; 10 = absolutely. Your challenge is to give real thought to their validity, and use what you have learned in this chapter to begin to question them and search for alternative possibilities. At the end of the book, you can re-rate them and see how much the strength of your beliefs has diminished.

---

3 Assumptions – the 'middle layer' of our thinking. Assumptions link our beliefs to our day-to-day thinking. In this sense, they are the 'middle layer' of our thinking. They also become our 'rules for living'.

For example, if you hold a negative belief that you are a boring person, then you may make an assumption that 'If I talk to people socially, they will find me dull and uninteresting.' When you receive a party invitation, you may think 'I won't go. No-one will want to talk to me.' Or you may go, but decide 'I'll just stand by myself in the corner and hope no one notices me. That way, I won't have to talk to people.'

Your 'rules for living'

You may develop a 'rule for living' not to socialize because you consider this will prevent your 'I am boring' belief being put to the test.

Anne, with her 'I'm not good enough' belief, might hold an assumption that 'If I stay on the bottom rung of the career ladder, doing simple work I can easily handle, then hopefully, I won't lose my job.' Anne is developing a rule for living that it is better not to do anything she finds difficult so that that her incompetence will never be discovered.

Identifying your rules

Can you identify any rules for living of your own? Look back at any basic beliefs that you managed to identify. Now ask yourself how you cope with those beliefs on a day-to-day basis. For instance, if you believe you are not especially likeable, your rule for living might be to be as nice as pie to everyone at all times to mitigate against this. Write down three rules for living that you tend to use to support some of your beliefs.

Our thoughts, assumptions and beliefs are not hard facts, and are often erroneous. It is not too hard to replace them with more helpful, accurate and positive alternatives.

Exercise 18

To help you identify the assumptions you make that guide your daily life, write down one or two recent self-defeating thoughts you may have had. Now see if you can work out what assumptions make that thought seem valid, and what basic belief might be lurking in the background. Do you have a rule for living to cope with this?

Evidence finding: don't let your emotional brain blind you to the facts

One of the problems people have with challenging negative, emotionally unintelligent thinking and replacing it with an idea that is more balanced and helpful is that the inclination is to still 'really believe' the negative thought.

Negative thoughts can be very hard to shift. It may take a great deal of practice to replace pessimistic beliefs with more constructive ones. A very helpful tool – thought by many to be the most important 'thought shifter' around – is to ask a simple question:

If this is really so, *where's the evidence?*

The case study opposite illustrates this.

Case study

Tom was very stressed at work and was really beginning to feel swamped and unable to cope. When he mentioned this to a colleague, Jim, his advice was to talk to his boss and explain the position. Tom said that he thought he couldn't do this as he was sure that his boss thought he wasn't up to the job and was looking to find a reason to get rid of him.

Tom felt more stressed than ever. Not only was he totally swamped with work that he felt he could not possibly complete on time, but now he had the worry that he might lose his job if he didn't. The extra stress caused his work rate to slow and more mistakes to appear.

When Jim popped his head around Tom's door he could see that Tom was in despair. 'Stop for a moment, Tom. Let's talk about this.'

'I don't have a moment,' said Tom. 'I'm so behind already and I'll get the sack if I don't finish this tonight.'

'Hold on there,' said Jim. 'Can I just ask you what happened two weeks ago when the Sales Awards were announced? Can I just ask you whose presentation brought in the biggest new client our company has had this year? And would you please tell me who has been recommended for the Senior Sales position when Peter retires in six months? Who is that?'

Tom blushed. 'Well, me, I guess,' he said sheepishly.

'And if you were your manager, would you give someone like that the sack, or would you be more likely to listen seriously to their problems and attempt to help them?'

'Well, the latter, I suppose,' said Tom.

'OK, then. What are your plans now?' asked Jim.

'I'll speak to my manager,' said Tom, with a rueful smile. 'Thanks, Jim. You have put things in perspective for me.'

This is what we mean by 'looking for evidence'. Tom's thinking had become so negatively skewed that he was discounting evidence that was staring him (or at least, his work colleague) in the face, which made it clear that his thinking was likely to be incorrect. Once he was forced to look for evidence to back up his thinking, he could find little – but there was a great deal to show that his thinking was incorrect.

Key point: 'Where's the evidence?' is one of the most important questions you will ever ask yourself to counteract pessimistic thinking. Never accept that your pessimistic thinking is 'spot on'. Always look for evidence to back it up – you may get a surprise when there is less evidence than you think!

Expanding your 'Thought record'

If you find the concept of using a 'Thought record' helpful (look back to page 67), then add in two additional columns as described below. This will give you excellent practice with 'Where's the evidence?' If you do put pen to paper, for the period you practise a new skill, rather than think 'I can do this in my head', it will always make your mind work harder and you will learn better.

Firstly, place a column next to your initial thoughts and write down any evidence you have to support it. Secondly, place a column next to your re-evaluated thoughts and ask yourself the same question. You will find, far more often than not, that you actually struggle to find evidence to support negative thinking, but quite a lot to support a more rational alternative. A good question to ask yourself is, 'In a Court of Law, what would the judge think of my evidence?' Evidence such as 'I just feel that way' or 'I assumed that when he/she said this, he/she meant that' just isn't good enough!

Exercise 19

To help you check the validity of your thinking, write down three situations over the last two weeks where you felt that your emotions got the better of you and that you handled things badly. Attempt to recall your thinking at those times. Draw a line down a page and write 'Where's the evidence?' at the top of the right-hand column.

Ideally, you are looking for evidence to dispute your negativity. However, don't worry if sometimes you have evidence to support your worries. Coping skills kick in then, which is just another way of being emotionally intelligent.

Making emotionally intelligent thinking your default

One question commonly asked in regard to EI is: Can such a thing really be developed, or are we simply 'born with it' (or not)? There is no doubt that genetic history and parenting style have a huge effect on our abilities to think and respond in certain predefined ways. Yet we are fortunate in the enormous capacity of the human brain to be open to new learning. The key is never to give up.

Imagine you are desperately trying to find a path through the jungle. No matter where you look, you can't see a way through. In the end, you decide to take your machete and simply hack through the undergrowth, which you gradually do. A while later, some others come through the same area of the jungle, also looking for a way through. Eventually, they see the thin trail you have hacked, and they tread the same path, cutting down more branches as they go. Soon, even more people come by, and they see the trail that is now beginning to develop. They use it themselves. Eventually, what was simply a thick jungle curtain has turned into a main thoroughfare – and it has happened due solely to usage. This is exactly how our brains work. Even when it has absolutely no past experience of mastering a skill, your brain will make an attempt at it and, provided you give it enough practice, it will eventually become a default way of thinking or doing something.

A simple model that helps to explain the process is the 'four stages of learning':

1 You start the process by being unconsciously incompetent. At this stage, you may have no awareness at all of how you think, feel or act, in relation to the impact this might make on personal life outcomes, or how others might think about us or respond to us. Most of us will know someone like this. 'How can he be so insensitive?' 'Doesn't she realize how ridiculous she looks?' 'Can't he see he'll never make friends if he behaves like that?' Actually, no, they can't see it. They are being unconsciously incompetent.

2 Then you become consciously incompetent. This stage is reached when you finally realize that you need to make some changes, but you are not quite sure how. You will have identified a weakness – or something that, even though okay, could be improved for better outcomes – and now you have to work out what you will do to achieve the result that you want. For example, if you have trouble relating to others, you may decide to join a social group to improve your conversational abilities, or perhaps purchase a self-help book on improving communication skills.

3 You become consciously competent. At this point, you are making changes and they are making a difference, but unless you think about them and focus on them, they don't happen. This is what being consciously competent means – it doesn't yet happen naturally.

This can be the stage at which many people give up. They are finding the efforts required too hard, and nothing happens without a lot of thought and effort. Like the gym membership you used every day and now rarely bother with, or the diet you started with great hope but which lasted only until you were offered a chocolate éclair – it's all an effort.

Provided you stick with it, however, there is good news. In the fourth stage of learning, you finally become ...

4 Unconsciously competent. You're there! No more effort. Suddenly you find yourself doing the things that will allow you to achieve the goals you set yourself, and you don't even have to think about it.

This is when the hard work all becomes worthwhile. Keep the four stages of learning in your mind for everything you attempt that is new and requires effort. It will hopefully encourage you to know that the major efforts are temporary, while the change for the better is permanent.

Key point: Understanding the 'four stages of learning' will increase your commitment to making an effort. It will come naturally in the end.

Exercise 20

To relate the four stages of learning to your own experience and learn from this, can you think of any examples of the four stages of learning that you have successfully used to make something 'stick'? Identify the different stages in reaching your goal. Can you recall times when you have reached stage 3 and given up, as the effort was all too much? What caused you to give up, and how might you prevent this happening again?

Experiencing one's self in a conscious manner – that is, gaining self-knowledge – is an integral part of learning.
Karen McCown, *Self-Science:*
The Emotional Intelligence Curriculum (1998)

Summary

Emotional self-awareness requires you to be able to manage your thoughts as they so strongly determine your emotions and your management of them. In this chapter we have explored how you can begin to do this, by being aware of the link between these components. Once you master these principles you can begin to manage your emotions much more easily.

- You have learned about faulty thinking. You may have been surprised by the number of different ways you can sabotage rationality. Once you become a victim of faulty thinking, you see the world differently and your emotions and behaviours will also be faulty – even though you may not realize it. You will now have an increased awareness of this. As you examine your automatic thoughts to check their validity, ask yourself, 'Which style of faulty thinking am I falling into by thinking in this way?'

- When we react to our emotions without especially identifying what they are and whether they are appropriate for the situation, our thinking can become quite unrealistic. The question 'Where's the evidence?' is one of the most powerful you can ever ask yourself as you make assumptions and act on them or react to them. Get used to using this tool, and your thoughts and emotions will become far more emotionally intelligent.

- Make it a habit to monitor and evaluate your self-talk. We referred to ensuring that what you have to say has value. Ensure that what you think has value as well. Don't waste your precious time and emotional resources on nonsense, or worry about things outside your control. Use your emotional energies wisely.

- Learning new skills – even just new ways of looking at life – is hard work and can take time. You now have a model – the four stages of learning – that you can use to identify where you are on the learning spectrum. Do remember that if you are struggling with a concept, the only reason for this is that you have not done it often enough, for long enough.

05

developing your personal core values

In this chapter you will learn:
- to identify your key personal values
- to understand the role of integrity in developing emotional intelligence
- skills for increasing your personal competency in emotionally intelligent core values.

Increasing personal competencies

You have now learned how to develop emotionally intelligent (EI) thinking skills. However, as mentioned in Chapter 04, our beliefs have a great effect on our day-to-day thinking. These beliefs – or core values – will define your thinking, your emotions and your behaviours. To be an emotionally intelligent person, you will need to have emotionally intelligent core values. In this chapter, we will look at what some of these are, and you will learn how to acquire or develop them.

Developing the qualities that will increase your EI will depend somewhat on your own views of what constitutes EI qualities and values. A good place to start is to look at some of those that have been widely identified as necessary to EI. Perhaps one of the most important competencies is integrity.

Integrity

> *Real integrity is doing the right thing, knowing that nobody's going to know whether you did it or not.*
>
> Oprah Winfrey, broadcaster

We all like to think we have integrity, and that our actions support it. But what exactly is it?

Integrity is action based on a consistent framework of principles. A person is said to have integrity to the extent that everything they do and believe is based on the same core set of values. While those values may change, it is their consistency with each other and with your actions that determine your integrity. Those with integrity are people whose words match what they do, and what they do reflects their values. They are dependable – they don't let you down. They are 100 per cent trustworthy. Integrity is the common denominator that sustains every other value you possess.

Think about the consequences of lack of integrity. If someone promises something and does not follow through, then the individual who was counting on them and put their faith in the person's word learns mistrust. That lack of trust may extend beyond the person who broke the promise and towards others as well. Lack of integrity is a double-edged sword. It cuts both the giver and the receiver. Both parties have lost. If the ripples of betrayal extend beyond the two people, many others can be affected.

The cost of broken words

In the case of a personal relationship, the cost of a broken word is more than just the loss of trust; it includes the inflicting of deep hurt on the person who was misled.

In business, a person's word has to be good. If you cannot be true to your word, you cannot be trusted and, when that happens, how can you continue to operate in business? Integrity is important at every level and in every aspect of society.

Integrity is something that has been taught throughout history. We can find the idea and importance of integrity emphasized in many religious teachings throughout every age of humans. Integrity is more than just an idea; it is a practical and necessary character trait that is required in order to have any lasting success in this world. (Of course it is true that some people achieve success quite deliberately through a serious lack of integrity, morals and ethics. However, the danger is that it is like a house built on shifting sand, and may well crumble sooner or later.)

Case study

Jane had arranged to have supper with a girlfriend. The friend had just been through a particularly unpleasant break-up with her partner and was extremely distressed. Jane, as one of her best friends, had suggested they go to one of their favourite restaurants, order a meal and some good wine, and Jane would provide listening and support for her friend to help her through this difficult period. However, a little later in the day, Jane received a call from someone she had dated a few times, inviting her to a rather glamorous media party – on the same evening that Jane was meeting her friend. Jane agonized. But the idea of dressing up to go out with a man she liked to an exciting venue won through, and Jane phoned her friend with an excuse about a business meeting and put her off.

What do you think about Jane's integrity? Jane, actually, was not a bad person – she had genuinely planned a kind thing for her distressed friend. The reason Jane let her down was that her values were not clear enough. Jane did not act with *responsibility* (to put her friend first as she had agreed), or with *kindness* (Jane's friend was in great need of her at that time). She did not act with *honesty* (it is quite possible that her friend may have understood completely had Jane told her the truth about her dilemma). Nor did Jane act with *courage* (she wasn't prepared to take the risk that her friend would be upset).

This may seem an insignificant story in many ways ('Oh, we've all done that at some point' may be a thought crossing your mind). However, it does raise a key point:

> **Key point:** If we wish to be emotionally intelligent, then acting with integrity at all times is a vital part of that.

Having integrity is about:

- being clear about your own values
- being open about your values to others
- behaving in a way that reflects the importance of your values to you.

Exercise 21

Below is an 'integrity scale' which, if you try it and respond with honesty, may make you think rather hard about your own integrity levels. Recall the common thought listed above, 'Oh, everybody does that some time'? Firstly, do they? Isn't it just those who lack integrity who do things like that? Secondly, such an attitude may creep into many aspects of a person's life who thinks that way. Which statement in each pair reflects (more often than not) an action closest to your own?

- I'm as good as my word./I often fail to do things I say I will do.
- I am straightforward with my dealings with others./I often have hidden agendas when dealing with others.
- I take responsibility for my actions./I try to off-load blame when something goes wrong.
- I am discreet./I enjoy a good gossip.
- I am consistent in my approach./I vary my approach, depending on circumstances.
- I maintain confidentiality./I sometimes tell unauthorized people confidential information.
- I am willing to tackle difficult issues./I avoid dealing with difficult issues.
- I talk about people in a positive way./I frequently run people down.
- I tell people assertively if I am unhappy./If someone does something I don't like, I don't say so though I may complain about them to others.

Source: *EI Advantage: Putting Emotional Intelligence into Practice*,
Patricia McBride and Susan Maitland (2004)

How to develop your integrity

Character is higher than intellect. A great soul will be strong to live as well as think.

Ralph Waldo Emerson, writer

Make some new rules

Depending on what you discovered when you did Exercise 21, you may wish to make some basic 'rules' for yourself that will increase your integrity levels in the future. Here are some suggestions, and you may like to add more.

Be 100 per cent trustworthy. This does not mean always doing what others want, but it means never saying 'Yes' when you mean 'No', and it means that, once you have given your word (even in an informal way), you don't break it. It doesn't mean that you cannot get things wrong and make errors. It means owning up and apologizing sometimes, rather than covering things up and making excuses.

Never break confidentiality. If you are the possessor of information given or written with the clear understanding that you do not pass it on, don't take it upon yourself to assess the importance of keeping or breaking that undertaking. It is not for you to decide that it doesn't really matter if you tell just one person. When someone tells you a secret, keep it. If you really doubt yourself, have the integrity to ask not to be given this confidential information in the first place.

Have courage in your beliefs and be open about them. If something doesn't seem quite right to you or if you find yourself in a situation where you feel uncomfortable with what is being asked or said – say so. (You may wish to work on your assertiveness skills if you find this difficult.)

Add some further 'rules' of your own. Now add some more ideas of your own. What can you do to develop your integrity further? Write down at least three further suggestions and then start to incorporate them into your daily life.

You can decide which of the core values, identified by Rogers (p. 43) and Goleman and Covey (p. 54), are the ones you personally hold dear. Take another look at these lists and think hard about which values you really wish to develop. To assist you, we will now look at some of them in more detail. As you work on one or two, you will find that as long as you understand the others – what they require and what they reflect in you – they will all begin to come naturally to you.

How to develop responsibility

It simply isn't possible to be emotionally intelligent without taking responsibility for your own actions. People who fail to take responsibility say things like:

'It's not my fault I am the way I am.'

'I never asked to be born.'

'Life is unfair. There is no sense in trying to take control of my life.'

'You can't help me, nobody can help me. I'm useless and a failure.'

'When do the troubles and problems cease? I'm tired of all this.'

'Life is so depressing. If only I had better luck and had been born to a healthier family, or attended a better school, or gotten a better job.'

'How can I be responsible for what happens to me in the future? Fate, luck and other negative influences have a greater bearing on my future than I have.'

'The problems in my family have influenced who I am and what I will be; there is nothing I can do to change that.'

'No matter how hard I work, I will never get ahead.'

'I am who I am; there is no changing me.'

Has there ever been a time when you have said or thought any of the above? Don't worry if your answer is a blushing 'yes' – we are all human and go through periods of self-pity where we feel that life is against us. Just acknowledging this, understanding it, and then acting to change it is all that EI asks of you.

Exercise 22

What does taking personal responsibility mean to you? Write down three or four ideas, and then look at the list below.

Accepting personal responsibility includes:

- acknowledging that you are solely responsible for the choices in your life
- accepting that you are responsible for what you choose to feel or think
- accepting that you choose the direction for your life

- accepting that you cannot blame others for the choices you have made
- realizing that you determine your feelings about any events or actions addressed to you, no matter how negative they seem
- recognizing that you are your best cheerleader; it is not reasonable or healthy for you to depend on others to make you feel good about yourself
- not feeling sorry for the 'bad hand' you have been 'dealt' but taking hold of your life and giving it direction and reason
- protecting and nurturing your health and emotional well-being
- taking an honest inventory of your strengths, abilities, talents, virtues, and positive points
- letting go of blame and anger towards those in your past who did the best they could, given the limitations of their knowledge, background and awareness.

Exercise 23

To help you increase your ability to take personal responsibility, think of an area in your life – at home, work or socially – where you have avoided taking responsibility for something. Now ask yourself the following questions:

- Why have I avoided taking responsibility over this?
- What outcomes resulted from my behaving in this way?
- Thinking now in terms of taking more personal responsibility, is there an alternative, more responsible way in which I could behave?

Do this exercise, either in your head or on paper, a few times. Then put it into action by increasing your personal responsibility in the weak areas you have identified.

How to develop openness

When we are short of self-esteem, the thought of being totally open with others is a frightening idea. A common view is that people will only like us if we hide certain aspects (many, even) of ourselves. We feel that we need to present ourselves in a certain way for others to like us, and that any sign of weakness will be harshly judged and criticized.

In reality, the opposite is true. Once we become willing to expose our weaknesses and fallibilities to others, we begin a process of true bonding. Consider for a moment who, of all your friends and acquaintances, you like the best. Those who always tell you how well things are going, how great their job is, how clever their children are, etc? I doubt it. Most likely, it will be someone who always 'says it as it is', and never tries to make anything sound either better or worse than it really is. We actually feel flattered by confidences – the person who will tell you about the bad things in their life, or instances of their personal failings, endear themselves to us. This is because we appreciate that they are not trying to present a 'public face'; they are just being themselves.

Once you realize how attractive this is to others, you may be willing to test it out.

Exercise 24

If you normally find it difficult to reveal something about yourself that you see as a negative trait, to help you practise disclosure make a real effort to do this with someone. Do this in a social situation rather than in the workplace where it may not go down well to disclose incompetencies, and be aware of the outcome. Think about the outcome you might expect. What actually happened? What feedback did you get from the person to whom you disclosed something? In most cases, your prediction will not match what actually happens. You will probably not expect an overly positive response, but you will almost certainly get one. People will admire you for being open, they will be sympathetic if there is a problem, and they will be quick to say, 'Hey, me too, I've had that happen and I've felt that way', and there is your bonding.

The more open you become, the more your confidence will grow. You will become used to talking intimately, and you will earn the respect of others.

Developing gratitude

The hardest arithmetic to master is that which enables us to count our blessings.

Eric Hoffer, writer

We neglect gratitude as a virtue at our peril. The results of various research shows conclusively that expressing gratitude increases our sense of happiness and well-being. Gratitude can simply be counting our blessings, or it can be an expression of appreciation to others that not only increases our own well-being, but theirs as well.

Psychologist Christopher Peterson has developed an exercise he calls 'Three good things'. Try this out and see how it works for you.

Exercise 25

To help you develop the value of gratitude, at the end of the day (not earlier), write down three things (no more) that went well. Also record why each event was a good one. (Peterson's rationale is that people are not especially mindful about good events unless they focus on them closely.) For most people, 'competency requires not comment' (Ryle, 1949) which means we usually assume that good things are our due. Accordingly, we do not think much about them and miss the potential benefits of thoughtful, conscious gratitude.

The three things on your list can be relatively small in importance: 'The milkman smiled at me.' 'Someone helped me when I dropped some papers on the floor.' Or they can be large in importance: 'I just got a major promotion.' However, large things tend to illicit thanks quite easily; it is the small things that we miss and that will make a real difference. For each positive event on your list, answer in your own words the question:

Why did this good thing happen?

For example, you might consider that the milkman smiled at you because you had bothered to say good morning, or simply because you consider that he finds you a nice person.

Do Exercise 25 for at least a week and evaluate whether there is an increase in your tendency to appreciate the small things in life – and what positive effect this has on you. Many people continue this exercise as a nightly habit. Eleanor Roosevelt was a known exponent of this, and I personally know a very happy, positive, emotionally intelligent woman who has written in her 'Golden Moments' notebook every night for 40 years.

It works!

Here are some suggestions for things you may neglect to be grateful for:

- a roof over your head
- your material possessions
- a car that runs
- your health
- your relationships
- your family
- your job
- your skills
- holidays.

A small warning

Often when people attempt to use gratitude, it's because they're actually feeling complacent or negative about their circumstances, but they're trying to look on the bright side and build some positive momentum. If you've ever expressed gratitude by starting with the words 'at least', you know what I mean. 'At least I have my health.' 'At least I have a roof over my head.' 'At least I have a holiday coming up.'

The underlying message is: 'What I have is OK, and I can temporarily feel grateful about it if I push myself to do so, but genuine gratitude isn't my default feeling because ultimately my circumstances just aren't that exciting. More often than not, they leave me feeling empty or complacent rather than grateful.'

However, even when your overall circumstances seem negative, you can still employ gratitude just by changing your focus. For example, instead of focusing on the negatives, you can say 'When I chose to do so, I can notice my life circumstances and feel grateful for them. I can feel grateful for my marriage, my children, my house, my career, my friendships' and so on. This type of gratitude is not dependent on situations and circumstances. It is a feeling of gratitude for life itself, for existence, for anything and everything you experience. With practice it becomes part of daily thinking.

> As we express our gratitude, we must never forget that the highest appreciation is not to utter words, but to live by them.
>
> John F. Kennedy, US President 1961–3

Holistic gratitude encompasses everything we have already spoken of, but goes beyond that to include being grateful for:

- your life
- the universe
- time and space
- your problems, challenges and hardships
- your foibles and mistakes
- your consciousness
- your ego
- your thoughts and emotions
- your freedom of choice
- ideas and concepts.

Circumstances are irrelevant because this form of gratitude is a choice that needs no justification. It is a sense of utter fascination with the very notion of existence. You become grateful for the adventure that is life, including all of its twists and turns. This form of gratitude is synonymous with unconditional love because there is no attachment to circumstances or outcomes. Consequently, there is no fear of loss or change.

When your feelings of gratitude are conditional upon temporary circumstances, such as your material possessions, your job, and your relationships, your basic character doesn't change significantly. But when you root your gratitude in something permanent, it becomes a permanent part of you. Instead of saying 'I am grateful for...' you just say 'I am grateful.'

> *Gratitude unlocks the fullness of life. It turns what we have into enough, and more. It turns denial into acceptance, chaos into order, confusion into clarity ... It turns problems into gifts, failures into success, the unexpected into perfect timing, and mistakes into important events. Gratitude makes sense of our past, brings peace for today and creates a vision for tomorrow.*
> Melodie Beattie, writer

Developing humility

> *Do you wish people to think well of you? Don't speak well of yourself.*
>
> Blaise Pascale, writer

You might question the importance or humility in your quest for EI. While the dictionary defines 'humility' as modesty, lacking pretence, and not believing that you are superior to others, an ancillary definition includes: 'Having a lowly opinion of oneself, meekness'.

Bruna Martinuzzi, an EI trainer from Canada, suggests, quite correctly, that we often confuse humility with timidity. Her belief is that humility is not clothing us in an attitude of self-abasement or self-denigration. Humility is about maintaining our pride about who we are, our achievements and our worth – but without arrogance. It is the antithesis of hubris, that excessive, arrogant pride that often leads to the derailment of some, as it does with the downfall of the tragic hero in the typical Greek drama. It's about a quiet confidence without the need for an overt selling of our wares. It's about being content to let others discover the layers of our talents without having to boast about them. It's a lack of arrogance, not a lack of aggressiveness in the pursuit of achievement.

It is interesting to notice that often the higher people rise and the more they have accomplished, the higher the humility index. Those who achieve the most, brag the least, and the more secure they are in themselves, the more humble they are. We have all come across people like that and feel admiration for them. Another mark of a person who practises humility is his or her treatment of others. Such people treat everyone with respect, regardless of position.

Something interesting happens, too, when we approach situations from a perspective of humility. It opens us up to possibilities because we choose open-mindedness and curiosity over protecting our point of view. We spend more time in that wonderful space of the beginner's mind, willing to learn from what others have to offer. We move away from pushing into allowing, from insecure to secure, from seeking approval to seeking enlightenment. We forget about being perfect and we enjoy being in the moment.

> *I long to accomplish a great and noble task, but it is my chief duty to accomplish humble tasks as though they were great and noble.*
>
> Helen Keller, writer

Key point: There are many benefits to practising humility. It improves relationships across all levels, it reduces anxiety, it encourages more openness and, paradoxically, it enhances one's self-confidence.

Exercise 26

Become more aware of your ability to practise humility by considering the following:

1 There are times when swallowing pride is particularly difficult, and any intentions of humility fly out the window as we become engaged in a contest of perfection, each side seeking to look good. If you find yourself in such no-win situations, consider developing some strategies to ensure that the circumstances don't lead you to lose your grace. Try this sometimes: just stop talking and allow the other person to be in the limelight. There is something very liberating in this strategy.

2 Here are three magical words that will produce more peace of mind than a week at an expensive retreat: 'You are right.'

3 Catch yourself if you benignly slip into preaching or coaching without permission – is zeal to impose your point of view overtaking discretion? Is your correction of others reflective of your own needs?

4 Seek others' input on how you are getting on in your leadership path. Ask: 'How am I doing?' It takes humility to ask such a question. And even more humility to consider the answer.

5 Encourage the practice of humility through your own example: every time you share credit for successes with others, you reinforce this ethos for others.

Source: Adapted from Bruna Martinuzzi,
Optimism: The Hidden Asset (2006)

Developing courage

It takes a lot of courage to release the familiar and seemingly secure, to embrace the new. But there is no real security in what is no longer meaningful. There is more security in the adventurous and exciting, for in movement there is life, and in change there is power.

Alan Cohen, writer

Courage takes many forms, and so it is different for each of us. I saw it last month in an old school friend who had to bury his mother two weeks before Christmas. There are also sisters of two friends who win awards of courage from me: one because when chemotherapy made her bald, she still kept her promise to volunteer at her daughter's school. She wore neither a wig nor a baseball cap; she carried a determination to show that life goes on. The other friend's sister has multiple sclerosis. I've lost count of the treatments she's agreed to try because, among other reasons, she wants to dance with her husband again. Do you think they consider themselves courageous? I doubt it. But they are, as all of us are every morning we get up. Every time we drive on the motorway or fly in an airplane, every time we say yes, or say no. It takes courage to walk into a room full of strangers, to give a speech, to have a baby, or to have none at all. It takes courage to fall in love, to learn a language, to hug like you mean it, to say goodbye. Courage is not necessarily the lack of fear. Courage, as John Wayne famously said, 'Is being scared to death – and saddling up anyway'.

Without courage, wisdom bears no fruit.

Baltasar Gracian, writer

In an emotionally intelligent life, the opposite of courage isn't fear. It's complacency. 'Oh, well,' we think. 'We've always smoked, why stop now?' Or we've thought about exercising, but our grandparents lived to be 90, so why do we need to sweat? We need to because life isn't about resting on our laurels or succumbing to our habits. It's about doing something that will make us better people – physically, mentally, emotionally – for ourselves and for those who love us.

Key point: It takes courage to set a goal, courage to work at it, courage to walk when we feel like sitting, to eat an apple when we want another doughnut.

Exercise 27

In developing emotional intelligence within ourselves, courage may mean… what?

List two situations you have ahead of you that frighten or concern you, and rate your ability to deal with them well. Perhaps you have to give someone some unpleasant news, or to tackle something you feel is beyond your capabilities. Perhaps it is facing up to something you have been ignoring for a while (that pile of bank statements, for example).

Now consider how you will deal with those situations to show courage. This doesn't mean dusting off a trusty sword, or tackling something aggressively. It means overcoming personal doubts and fears, and showing strength in standing by your principles. This is everyday courage in action. It is not about absence of fear, but the awareness that something else is more important. It is not only the type of courage that can be displayed in visible, heroic ways, but the quiet, private battles we fight when attempting to overcome inner fears.

Moral excellence comes about as a result of habit. We become just by doing just acts, temperate by doing temperate acts, courageous by doing courageous acts.
Aristotle, Greek philosopher

Developing motivation

Many of life's failures are people who did not realise how close they were to success when they gave up.
Thomas Edison, inventor

As human beings, we are goal-oriented, and being self-motivated means pursuing our goals with commitment, passion, energy and persistence. In order to achieve high levels of motivation, overcome setbacks and perform at our best, we need to be able to manage our own internal states, harness our emotions and channel them in a direction that enables us to achieve our objectives.

While integrity is the driver of other emotionally intelligent values, self-motivation is the driver of achieving these to the best of your abilities. Motives are what cause us to act – otherwise, why bother? The fact that you are reading this book means that you are motivated in at least some way to discover more about IE. You may be motivated to develop it and are seeking ways to do this.

Emotions motivate our behaviour in ways that are adaptive and helpful to us. Just as an emotion directs our attention to an event, it can motivate and inspire us. Emotions are not passive.

They have an action component or tendency; they are indicators and motivators of our needs and wants.

Why you need motivation

- You cannot always rely on others to encourage you. If you have positive friends who are always there when you need them then you are indeed lucky but you cannot always count on this. Often, when you face any difficulties in your life you must rely on your own motivation to get you through.
- You need self-motivation to achieve your goals. This is what gives you the ability to encourage yourself to accept opportunities and challenges.
- You need self-motivation to plan and find a broader direction in your life.

Psychologist Abraham Maslow suggested that our needs form a hierarchical pyramid, with our basic needs (warmth, food, freedom from fear) at the bottom, and our intellectual and spiritual needs at the top. His view is that we only become motivated to achieve a need further up the pyramid once the previous, lower need has been met. (See *Motivation and Personality*, Maslow, 1987)

Maslow's hierarchy of needs

Self-actualization needs

growth, accomplishment, personal development

Self-esteem needs

self-respect, status, recognition

Social needs

belonging, acceptance, social life, friendship, love

Safety needs

security, protection from danger

Physiological needs

hunger, thirst, sleep

Studies of EI show that when we are acting in an emotionally unintelligent way, we are likely to be focusing on one or more of our lower needs.

In order to motivate yourself at the higher levels of the hierarchy, you must give more significance to your thinking, feeling and behaviour. This brings us back to the notion of personal awareness.

- Learn to think positively by seeking the positive aspects of a situation before considering the alternatives.
- Learn to recognize which of your feelings are emotional, which are physiological and which are intuitive.
- Instead of asking, 'Why has this happened?' ask, 'What can I do to change it?'

How we become motivated by emotion

Every time you are enticed into adopting a new behaviour, you are motivated by the effects of emotion. Where emotion is induced by a brief and dramatic experience, you cannot count on it to create lasting change. For example, you may be watching television and are moved by an appeal for people to give blood, or to help refugees in a country plagued with famine. Your motivation to do something about it immediately afterwards may be very high, but it is unlikely to be sustained.

> **Key point:** Self-motivation must encompass practice. You must train your brain to adopt new, more emotionally intelligent ways of thinking and acting, and that only comes with practice.

As you learn new strategies for improving your EI, remember that practise makes perfect. You won't increase your EI simply by deciding to do things differently. Practise is what will strengthen the pathway between your emotions and your reason. Repetition of new, more emotionally intelligent behaviours will increase your motivation to acquire skills that are lasting and enduring, rather than transient.

> **Key point:** Will-power alone will never work over the long term. It is the hardest way possible to get yourself to do anything. Instead, you need to tap into the limitless power of your mind. When you do this, you can break bad habits, create beneficial new ones and put yourself back on track easily, quickly and with very little effort.
>
> Forget about will-power; become a self-motivation expert.

Exercise 28

To help you work on self-motivation, write down one small action you have been putting off and answer the following questions. Really put some thought into the answers.

1 What am I missing out on of importance by not doing this?
2 What will I gain most by doing this?
3 Why is it important to me to do this?
4 How is not doing this inconsistent with who I really am?

And then, pretend that you have already completed the action. Take five minutes to write down how you feel now that you have already finished the task you have been postponing, i.e. as if you have already succeeded. Do this quickly and write with as much emotion as you can express.

For example, I have already cleaned the yard and I feel fantastic. My family and friends are really impressed and I feel so proud of myself and so delighted that it is finally done. The yard looks immaculate, so tidy I have even impressed myself. I feel so powerful, energetic and motivated. I feel on top of the world.

You will be surprised at how well this simple process works. You may find that you feel a boost in motivation that gets even better each time you use this process. Do it once a day for best results.

Summary

This chapter has focused on developing EI personal competencies. To do this, you first need to choose your own personal values – those that are particularly important and pertinent to you.

- Developing these values relies first of all on your integrity – a consistent framework of principles that you can then apply 'across the board'. Understanding the importance of integrity, and the consequences of lack of integrity, has been an integral part of your learning in this chapter.
- Further key competencies – taking responsibility, openness, humility and gratitude – are all components of emotionally intelligent thinking and behaviour.
- You will achieve little without self-motivation. This means setting goals that you are keen to achieve, and seeing the purpose in the practice you are undertaking. Stephen Covey describes this well when he refers to 'beginning with the end in mind' (*Seven Habits of Highly Effective People*, 1989).

06

emotional
intelligence and
resilience

In this chapter you will learn:
- the importance of resilience
- the call of resilience on your emotions
- the characteristics of resilience
- how emotional intelligence will help you develop resilience.

The things that go right in our lives predict future successes, and the things that go wrong do not damn us forever.

Kirk Felsman, psychologist

We have now looked at several of the core values that will help you to develop your emotional intelligence. Now you need to learn how to become resilient. This is one of the basic characteristics of EI – the ability to stand firm in the face of adversity, and to be able to respond strongly to emotions that might be upsetting or difficult to deal with. Resilience will help you to manage your emotional responses and ensure that they are appropriate to the situation you are in. This chapter will teach you the skills to achieve this.

How resilient are you?

When something goes wrong, do you bounce back or do you fall apart? People with resilience harness inner strengths and tend to rebound more quickly from a setback or challenge, whether it's a job loss, an illness or the death of a loved one. To be resilient, you must also be emotionally intelligent, and to be emotionally intelligent, you must be resilient.

In contrast, people who are less resilient – with lower levels of EI – may dwell on problems, feel victimized, become overwhelmed and turn to unhealthy coping mechanisms, such as substance abuse. They may even be more inclined to develop mental health problems. Resilience won't necessarily make your problems go away, but it can give you the ability to see past them, find some enjoyment in life and better handle future stressors.

If you aren't as resilient as you'd like, you can teach yourself to become more resilient.

Resilience can be an asset in times of real hardship

There is a great deal of research being carried out worldwide into resilience, what it means, and how it can be fostered and developed. While most of you reading this book will have an interest in resilience as part of developing an emotionally intelligent personality, there are people all over the world, especially children, whose lives – usually through no fault of their own – are quite horrendous. Civil war, hunger, or lack of the most basic resources such as clean water, require people to survive in the face of enormous difficulties. Resilience in these circumstances can make the difference between death and survival, and this is why research is being carried out. Being able to teach this skill to people will help them immeasurably.

You can benefit from resilience as much as someone in deprived circumstances

While the impetus for resilience research has been primarily to help deprived and disadvantaged people to survive in poor circumstances, what has emerged is an idea of resiliency that is important to emotional good health and is relevant to us all.

Some definitions of resilience

To help you understand it better, here are some definitions of resiliency, as it has been defined by a variety of researchers in the field:

- 'Remaining competent despite exposure to misfortune or stressful events.'
- 'A capacity that allows a person to prevent, minimize or overcome the damaging effects of adversity.'
- 'The capacity some people have to adapt successfully despite exposure to severe stressors.'
- 'The human capacity to face, overcome and even be strengthened by the adversities of life.'
- 'The process of, capacity for, or outcome of successful adaptation despite challenging or threatening circumstances.'

Exercise 29

Having read these definitions, are you able to come up with one of your own that would best describe what resilience (or a stronger dose of it) might mean for you? Write it down.

Can you now think of any situations or difficulties in your life, either now or in the recent past, where resilience as you have described it above would be of help to you? What difference to the outcome might resilience make, or have made? Again, jot down your thoughts. (Remember, as we mentioned in Chapter 04, writing things down is a much more powerful way of thinking about them, than simply trying to run them through in your head).

Understand what having good resilience can give you

Resilience means using your emotions to adapt to stress and adversity

Resilience is the ability to adapt well to stress, adversity, trauma or tragedy. It means that, overall, you remain stable and maintain healthy levels of psychological and physical functioning in the face of disruption or chaos.

Resilience helps you to cope with temporary disruptions in your life and the challenges they throw up. For instance, you may have a period when you worry about an elderly parent who is sick. Resilience ensures that, despite your concerns, you're able to continue with daily tasks and remain generally optimistic about life.

EI is vital in enhancing resilience because it means more than merely trying to weather a storm. It doesn't mean you ignore feelings of sadness over a loss – it actually means, in EI terms, becoming *more* aware of them, and then being able to deal with them. It does not mean that you always have to be strong and that you can't ask others for support – in fact, reaching out to others is a key component of nurturing resilience in yourself.

- Resilience doesn't mean that you're unable to express your emotions or that you don't feel them.
- Resilience can provide protection against emotional disorders such as depression and anxiety. It will help individuals deal constructively with the after-effects of trauma.
- Resilience may even help strengthen you against certain physical illnesses such as heart disease and diabetes.
- People who are resilient have the ability to say to themselves, 'This disaster has occurred, but I have a choice. I can either dwell on it or I can do something about it.'

Resilience gives you the skills to endure hardship

Resilience can help you to endure loss, stress, traumas and other challenges. It will enable you to develop many internal resources that you can draw upon to help you survive challenges and to thrive in the midst of chaos and hardship.

Resilient individuals are able to cultivate a sense of acceptance (which is not the same thing as defeatism) and, regardless of the setback, they can let go of it and move on.

Learning the characteristics of resilience

American psychologist and researcher Nancy Davis identified six areas of competence that she defined as characteristics of resilience.

Exercise 30

To help you think about your present level of resilience, read through the characteristics below and think hard about those that may already apply to you, or where they don't yet, whether you could absorb them and develop them yourself.

How did you get on? You will no doubt be familiar with many of the competencies as we have described them in previous chapters as essential for the development of good EI.

Physical

- Good health
- Easy temperament.

Spiritual

- Having faith that one's own life matters
- Seeing meaning in one's life even in pain and suffering
- Sense of connection with humanity.

Moral

- Ability and opportunity to contribute to others
- Willingness to engage in socially and/or economically useful tasks.

Emotional

- Ability to identify and control emotions
- Ability to delay gratification (patience)
- Realistically high self-esteem
- Creativity
- Sense of humour.

Social/relational

- Ability to form secure attachments
- Basic trust
- Ability and opportunity to actively seek help from others
- Ability to make and keep good friends
- Ability to empathize
- Possess good other-awareness.

Cognitive (thinking skills)

- Possess high EI
- Possess good communication skills
- Be open to a variety of ideas and points of view
- Have a capacity to plan
- Be able to exercise foresight
- Possess good problem-solving abilities
- Be able to take and use initiative
- Possess good self-awareness
- Be able to appreciate and assess the consequences of actions taken.

Source: Adapted from Davis (1999)

It is crucial to remember that, given an adequate facilitating environment, people have the capacity for positive change and for the development of at least some characteristics of resilience throughout their lives.

Nancy Davis, psychologist

Key point: In a sense, wherever we look, we come back to the same core skills and competencies that we either have, or need to develop, which measure our EI levels.

Exercise 31

Here is a test to measure your resiliency – your ability to bounce back from stressful situations. It is based on discovering the level of characteristics you possess that make people more resilient. For example, flexibility, self-confidence, creativity, and an ability to learn from experience.

Look at each statement below, and note down the number (from 1 to 5) that most closely describes how much you agree with it.

1 = strongly disagree; 5 = strongly agree

1 I don't allow difficulties to get me down for long. ☐

2 I am able to be open about my feelings; I don't harbour grievances and I don't get downhearted easily. ☐

3 I am normally confident and possess good self-esteem. ☐

4 If things go wrong, I am able to stay calm and work out the best course of action. ☐

5 I'm optimistic that any difficulties presented are temporary and I expect to overcome them. ☐

6 I usually adapt to changes in circumstances quickly and without fuss. ☐

7 My positive emotions are strong enough to help me move on from setbacks. ☐

8 I can be quite creative in thinking up solutions to problems. ☐

9 I normally trust my intuition and it usually serves me well. ☐

10 I am curious, ask questions and I am keen to know how things work. ☐

11 I am generally at ease with myself. ☐

12 I'm a good problem solver and enjoy the challenges that problems present. ☐

13 I can usually find something to laugh about, even in the direst situations. ☐

14 I am able to be self-effacing and laugh at myself. ☐

15 I always try to find something positive to learn from my experiences. ☐

16 I'm usually good at understanding other people's feelings. ☐

17 I am flexible, and can usually adapt fairly quickly to situations as they change. ☐

18 I try to look ahead and anticipate and, if possible, deflect problems before they happen. ☐

19 I usually consider myself to be strong and independent, and I don't tend to give in when things are difficult. ☐

20 I'm open-minded about other people's views and lifestyles. ☐

21 I am not constantly anxious when things are uncertain. ☐

22 I don't usually fail at tasks I am presented with, provided they are reasonably within my capabilities. ☐

23 I regard myself, and believe others regard me, as a good leader. ☐

24 I believe that experiencing difficult situations can make me stronger. ☐

25 I believe that something good comes out of every bad thing. ☐

Scores

100–120 You are extremely resilient.

76–99 You normally bounce back quite well.

50–75 You may wobble occasionally.

Under 50 You find recovery from difficulties quite hard and you need to develop your personal strength to deal with what life throws at you.

Don't worry if your resilience ratings weren't as high as you'd hoped or expected. It is not hard to develop the qualities that will improve your resilience in all areas of your life.

Learning how to manage your emotions by improving your resilience

Exercise 32

Take a pen and paper and, as you read on, make a written note of any of the points that you that you may need to work on. Keep this by you to use later in the chapter with further exercises.

Having checked your score on the rating scale for Exercise 31, what do you think you may need to do to improve your resilience? Write down some ideas.

Here are some further suggestions for improving your resilience that you may find helpful.

- Look back at other times in your life when you have had to cope with difficulties – perhaps something you felt you would not be able to overcome. What actually happened? What helped you to resolve the situation? Was there anything that didn't help? If so, ensure that you don't repeat that mistake. Building on the way you coped well with previous difficult situations will increase your resilience when you are faced with a new problem. Think also about how you may have changed as a result of dealing with the difficulty. Reflect on this. Are you perhaps stronger than you thought? If you really don't think so – if you feel worse as a result of your experiences – then consider what changes you might make to improve things next time.

- Build strong, positive relationships with your family and friends. These relationships provide mutual support in times of difficulty, which will help your own resilience and help you to offer this to others. Becoming involved in groups and/or charity work is also helpful. The power of the group, both to nurture you and give you support, is enormous. Groups also ensure that you will never feel alone during tough times.

- Use your thought-challenging skills. Even when things seem quite dire, constantly ask yourself whether there is a more positive way that you can look at things. If you can encourage yourself to remain hopeful and optimistic when you're in the middle of a crisis, it will be much easier to get through. Resilience is not always about putting things right, but about taking an optimistic view even when you cannot change events.

- When you can, trying to find the funny side of things will always strengthen you – as well as relaxing you in a tense situation. Of course, this is sometimes extremely hard, but seeing the funny side doesn't mean you are not taking things seriously – it simply means that when emotions come to the fore, positive emotions will keep you stronger than negative ones. The idea that being angry and distressed is somehow more helpful than being good-humoured is, of course, unfounded.

- Never forget the basics. Your personal ability to develop resilience will depend a great deal on looking after yourself. Make sure that your diet is healthy, you exercise regularly, perhaps practise relaxation exercises or take a yoga class, take care of your appearance and make plenty of time for activities that you enjoy. Nurturing your mind and body in this way will keep you mentally, as well as physically, strong. Having a sense of personal well-being strengthens your belief that you can tackle difficulties and overcome them.

- Develop a philosophy of acceptance. Be flexible. Few things stay the same, and it is often hard to anticipate changes that may affect your life – sometimes quite drastically. If you can be open-minded about life events, you will upset yourself less and you will have far more energy to face and, if necessary, tackle changes. You will adapt more easily and see the positive side of new events, rather than grieving for what has passed.

- Do something every day that gives you a sense of accomplishment and achievement. This may be something you really don't want to do for a variety of reasons, but pushing yourself to face up to it and get on with it will strengthen you and make you feel good. Get into a regular habit. Don't discourage yourself by focusing on tasks that seem unachievable. Instead, ask yourself, 'What's one thing I know I can accomplish today that helps me move in the direction I want to go?'

- With chronic problems, stop wishing and hoping that they will go away, and take some action to put them right. Many of us spend a great deal of time and energy on simply wishing things would change. Wishing that your problems will go away doesn't usually work and wastes a lot of valuable time when you could be actually doing something about them. Take decisive action rather than detaching yourself from problems and stresses. Once you address your problems with an action plan, you are on the way to overcoming them.

- Be proud of yourself. Think in positive terms about your abilities and strengths, and mentally encourage yourself to face problems with confidence. Believe you can do it. Positive self-talk is often brushed aside as meaning little – in fact it is a very powerful tool. The more you tell yourself that you are capable and strong, that you can withstand difficulties and criticism, the more control you will have over events and situations in your life and confidence in your ability to manage them well.

- Everything is relative. Sometimes we see our problems in isolation rather than against the bigger picture of the world around us. This can negatively discourage us as we may see our difficulties as acute and overwhelming. Look around you and evaluate your problems against those of the wider world – and perhaps even against those you have weathered before. Once you get a better perspective, your problem will become easier to resolve.

Consider keeping a personal journal and writing about your deepest thoughts and feelings relating to the events that have happened to you. This can be a very good way of learning to express your emotions, with the bonus of privacy. Trying meditation or other more spiritual, rather than practical, ways forward can be of help to some people.

Certain circumstances are impossible to correct, and you cannot change the fact that they have happened, and have had an adverse effect on your life. In such circumstances, resilience offers you the chance to respond in the most positive way you can. This may simply be acceptance and forgiveness, or it may be an ability to learn and adapt in the best way you can. Sometimes, accepting circumstances that cannot be changed can help you to focus on other things that you can alter.

Always remember that something good comes out of every bad thing. You may learn something about yourself that is valuable and positive after disaster. You may have become stronger through tragedy, or become closer to others who have shared your experience. Resilience grows from facing hardship, and this is a positive result for you. Many people who have faced disaster report on a heightened appreciation of life afterwards and a greater sense of joy from simply being alive.

Always focus on solutions, rather than problems. This will give you an active focus, rather than a passive one. Think in solution-focused mode and determine not to dwell on the negative side of the situation.

The most important thing is to identify ways that are likely to work well for you as part of your own personal strategy for fostering resilience. So now write these down.

Three sources of resilience

The International Resilience Project (which is undertaking the resilience research mentioned earlier in this chapter) defines resiliency in terms of three sources, which it labels: 'I have' (social and inter-personal supports), 'I am' (inner strengths) and 'I can' (inter-personal and problem-solving skills).

Exercise 33

To help you discover whether you have – or need to create – the three sources of resilience, take a look at each of the sources and make a note of those strengths that you personally consider to be already present in your life.

I have:

- people around me who I trust and who love me no matter what
- people who set limits for me so I know when to stop before there is danger or trouble
- people who show me how to do things correctly by the way they do things
- people who want me to learn to do things on my own
- people who help me when I am sick, in danger or need to learn.

I am:

- a person people can like and love
- glad to do nice things for others and show my concern
- respectful of myself and others
- willing to be responsible for what I do
- sure things will be all right.

I can:

- talk to others about things that frighten or bother me
- find ways to solve problems I face
- control myself when I feel like doing something that is not right or dangerous
- figure out when it is a good time to talk to someone or to take action
- find someone to help me when I need to.

According to Grotberg, for a person to be resilient, they need to have more than one of these strengths. For example, if a child has plenty of self-esteem (I am), but lacks someone they can turn to for support (I have), and does not have the capacity to solve problems (I can), they will not be resilient.

Look at the strengths you have noted down. Are they spread well across the three main sources? This will indicate higher resilience than if they are bunched together under one source.

Understanding resiliency as a developing process

Resiliency is not a personal attribute because this would imply a fixed and unchanging strength that some have and some do not. It is a more complex process involving internal cognitive (thinking) and personality factors and external protective factors. Resiliency is also a normal, understandable process. It arises from normal, human qualities such as the ability to rationally solve problems, the capacity to regulate emotion and the ability to form close, supportive ties with others. It is only when these systems are damaged or overwhelmed that natural resiliency fails. In other words, it goes hand in hand with EI. By developing one, you develop the other.

Thinking your way into being more resilient

Exercise 34

To develop personal resilience in specific areas, you will need to practise.

Write down four aspects of your life in which you consider yourself to be resilient in general, or you have specifically shown resilience recently (use the list you made from page 100).

Now do the same for areas of your life where you consider you would like to develop your resilience.

When you look at the parts of your life where you have shown resilience, what specific attributes have you shown – for example, tenacity, emotional control, ability to see the problem and the solution? Use examples from what you have read so far to give yourself some ideas. Now write them down.

Look at the areas of your life where you would like to develop your resilience. Would any of the attributes you have identified already help you? If not, what further attributes would you need to develop (again, look for examples in what you have read so far).

How can you develop attributes to help your resilience? Here's how. Developing resilience means, most importantly, stepping outside of your comfort zone. It means being willing to try a little harder, carry on when you might previously have given up, and being willing to feel emotions, such as anxiety and fear, and yet not back down. It also means practice. The only reason most people do not master new skills as well as they would like is that they simply have not done them often enough for long enough. Keep practising, and the difficult becomes possible, and the possible becomes easy.

Developing resilience also means positive self-talk. American psychologist Christine Padesky, who has spent some time researching and developing a model for improving resilience, has compiled a list of 'summary statements' that give a positive lift to resilience competencies, for example:

Area of resilience competency	Suggested summary statement
Having a problem-solving attitude	These are simply problems to solve
Having a problem-solving strategy	If I break this down into smaller pieces I will be able to handle it better
Being persistent	If I just stick at it and I don't give up I will be able to work something out
Finding an inspirational metaphor	For example, a stream running over stones, over time, will actually wear them down
Having a tenacious attitude	No matter what, I'll find another way
Being flexible	I will find some different perspectives on the problem
Using social support	Others are there to help me if I ask
Having emotional resilience	Even though I feel ..., over time I know I can find a way to cope
Developing a spiritual focus	I will focus on what is important and keep calm and focused
Connect with others	I am not alone – other people struggle with this as well
Focus on success instead of failure	It helps if I focus on how far I have come or what I have been able to do so far
See challenges instead of problems	I can be more creative and flexible here
Focus on possibilities not difficulties	Rome wasn't built in a day

Use humour	Hmmm ... this isn't going to be as easy as it looks!
Develop acceptance	Maybe things can't always go the way I want
Take an active approach	Make a list of options and consider them all

Source: Adapted from *Uncover Strengths and Build Resilience: A Four Step Model*, Christine Padesky, 2007

Learn the factors in resilience

A combination of factors contributes to resilience. As stated earlier, it is not one individual attribute, but a process involving both internal cognitive and personality factors and the development of external, helpfully protective factors such as a supporting family. Relationships that create love and trust, provide role models, and offer encouragement and reassurance help bolster your resilience.

Resilience helps your confidence and management of emotions

Several additional factors are associated with resilience, including:

- the capacity to make realistic plans and take steps to carry them out
- a positive view of yourself and confidence in your strengths and abilities
- skills in communication and problem solving
- the capacity to manage strong feelings and impulses.

All of these are factors that people can develop within themselves. Now think about your personal strategies for building resilience to manage your emotions. Developing resilience is a personal journey. People do not all react in the same way to traumatic and stressful life events. An approach to building resilience that works for one person might not work for another; people use varying strategies. Some variations may reflect cultural differences, as a person's culture might impact on how they communicate feelings and deals with adversity – for example, whether and how a person connects with significant others, including extended family members and community resources. With growing cultural diversity, the public has greater access to a number of different approaches to building resilience.

Think about what being resilient means to you, and identify the areas of your life where a more resilient outlook might be helpful to you. Your other learning about EI is all part of developing resilience. It will fit together well and increase your EI competencies generally.

Summary

In this chapter you have learned about the importance of resilience as a core value in developing EI.

- Resilience is a cornerstone of EI, and goes hand in hand with it.
- If you are to manage your emotions, you must develop resilience so that you can remain emotionally intelligent in adversity. EI is not something that works simply when things are going well.
- In this chapter you will have recognized a variety of characteristics present in a resilient personality, some of which you may have already, and others you may have identified and feel that you can now develop.
- Work with those areas that apply to you. You will have noticed the role that self-confidence plays, and you may decide that you need to work on this as well.
- Remember that we all react differently to traumatic and stressful events. There is no one right way, but managing your emotions in the face of adversity will ensure that whatever way you choose will be appropriate for you.

07

using emotional intelligence to defeat anger

In this chapter you will learn:
- to identify your anger triggers
- to discriminate between healthy and unhealthy anger
- to control your unhealthy anger
- to replace anger with more constructive ways of achieving your aims.

When managing our emotions seems too hard

Anybody can become angry, that is easy; but to be angry with the right person, and to the right degree, and at the right time, and for the right purpose, and in the right way, that is not within everybody's power, that is not easy.

Aristotle, Greek philosopher

Emotional intelligence is all about being aware of our emotions, identifying them, and then controlling them. But what if we can't? What if, no matter how many books we read and seminars we attend, when push comes to shove, the moment we find ourselves riled, the emotional brain takes over and we 'lose it'?

I work with many clients who are good, decent, caring people. Yet anger seems to be the one emotion that they cannot control. This 'anger habit' includes the tendency to experience temper tantrums, feelings of ongoing frustration, resentment and irritability. Of all the emotions, with the exception of passionate love, anger seems to be the hardest to control.

Can you be emotionally intelligent if you cannot control your anger? We all know people who have the kindest of hearts, and who are emotionally very open, yet their one obvious weakness is that they get angry very quickly. Getting angry doesn't make you a bad person – but it does mean that you are unnecessarily on the losing end of a great many situations. If you find yourself getting angry, quite quickly, a lot of the time, you have a problem and need to deal with it.

High anger can ruin both personal and professional relationships, as well as be detrimental to your health. At its worst, anger can also kill. Road rage is an example of this. An otherwise rational man or woman becomes so angry with another driver's behaviour that they decide to get their own back by giving chase. An accident results that kills two of the people involved. There may have been many reasons for this crazy, destructive behaviour – too much to do, setting off late, not allowing enough time to get from A to B, generally feeling that people are inconsiderate – but it was the inability to manage the emotion of high anger that resulted in the tragedy.

Twenty-first-century intolerance

We are more concerned than ever with our rights (fuelled, very often, by a compensation culture). We are less philosophical, less inclined to 'put things down to experience'. If our demands are not now met in a way that we have come to expect, we become angry. As we become generally angrier – so do others. This means it takes a lot less for us to get into a fight with someone, or to be provoked ourselves.

Suppressing anger

Expressing anger, especially in the workplace, is becoming less and less acceptable. This means that by expressing anger inappropriately we may risk our job, or at least disciplinary action. We might be sued by someone who feels that we have exhibited aggression towards them. We therefore often bottle anger up, instead of dealing with it, and this can be exceedingly harmful to both our emotional and physical well-being.

> *If you do not wish to be prone to anger, do not feed the habit; give it nothing which may tend to its increase.*
>
> Epictetus (55 AD–135 AD)

Me? Angry?

We all have different views on what is acceptable and what is not when it comes to anger. What may seem an angry response to person A is a natural way of dealing with situations for person B.

Exercise 35

Are you aware of your own anger? Answer the following questions to check it out. Score your answers: 0 = never, 1 = occasionally, 2 = often.

1 Others comment on my aggressive responses.

2 Waiting in queues drives me mad.

3 I can't tolerate rudeness.

4 I always respond badly to criticism.

5 I start arguments easily.

6 Driving in traffic causes me huge stress.

---

7 I consider most other drivers on the road to be bad drivers.

8 I find most shop assistants and helplines, etc. quite incompetent.

9 In difficult discussions with people, I tend to get angry the most quickly.

10 I let petty annoyances really work me up.

Scores

0–7: Don't worry; you stay well balanced in most tricky situations.

8–14: You are responding to stressful situations with anger too often.

15–20: Your angry responses may cause some serious damage if you don't make urgent changes.

If you scored highly in Exercise 35, don't worry – you can make changes to calm down your anger. Simply accepting the reality that you do get inappropriately angry is half the battle to reducing such responses.

The word 'inappropriate' is important here. Anger is not always a bad thing. It can often be emotionally intelligent to get angry. The key to this is being able to *control* your anger, and to use it only when it is appropriate, while containing it when it is not.

When is anger good?

Exercise 36

What would you say the differences are between healthy, constructive, emotionally intelligent anger and unhealthy, destructive anger?

Have you ever thought of anger as being a good, emotionally intelligent thing? If not, think about it for a moment, and write down three or four suggestions as to when it might be.

Let's take a look at some possibilities of anger as a good, emotionally intelligent action.

Anger at injustice

You see someone kicking a dog, hear on the news that innocent people in a far off country are being brutally treated, notice

someone at work who is always unfairly picked on by the boss...
These are situations where injustice prevails, and we need to get
angry about these things. World starvation, unnecessary wars,
people dying through lack of health care – the only way to get
anything done about such situations is for at least some of us to
feel very angry about them.

Anger to get results

As an absolutely last resort, if you really need to get results from
recalcitrant staff, motor mechanics, waiters, your children, etc.
then reasonable anger can work a treat.

Anger as a motivational tool

When you finally hear yourself (or someone else) say 'Right.
That's it. I'm not taking any more of this', you know that either
you (or they) are going to blow their top in order to get some
action. In a sense, you are bringing some energy to the situation.

Anger as a release

'Letting it all out' has actually been shown to have health
benefits, compared to repressed anger that we hold inside and
which eats away at us. However, there are ways of letting things
out that don't involve becoming apoplectic, so use this release
with caution.

Anger as an alert signal

Healthy anger can let you know that something is wrong. You
can use this alert to work out what is worrying you, and then do
something positive to change it. For example, if you find
yourself becoming irritated every time you need to meet with a
particular work colleague, ask yourself why they annoy you so.
It may be that they are always late for your meetings, always
dominate the discussion or regularly cancel at the last minute.
Becoming aware of your anger in these circumstances
encourages you to change the situation so that it is less stressful.

The point of taking a look at healthy anger is to bring home to
you that you do not need to eliminate this emotion from your
life. Anger can be a good emotion, but in appropriate
circumstances. Inappropriate anger is a problem.

> **Key point:** Don't attempt to eliminate anger from your life – there are many ways in which healthy anger can be a helpful and motivating tool.

Exercise 37

To help discover whether your own anger is healthy or not, think of two or three situations in which you became angry in the last week or so. Now think for a moment about the outcome. Do you feel that, in any of these instances, your anger had achieved a good result? If so, what was it? Do you feel that your anger was an emotionally intelligent response in these circumstances?

Where anger comes from

Anger stems from our expectations regarding the ideals and behaviours of others. We expect people to treat us fairly and they don't. We expect them to be nice to us and they aren't. We expect them to help us and they walk away.

Each time someone breaks a rule of ours, violates a contract or acts against our wishes, a possible option is to react with anger. We do not absolutely have to – it is our choice. Unfortunately, we do not always feel that we are in control of this choice – we feel unable to manage our emotions and it is as though it has already been decided for us and we act accordingly.

Earlier in this book (see Chapter 04), we did a lot of work on emotionally intelligent thinking. You now need to use the skills you have learned to help you to manage and reduce your angry thoughts and feelings.

The anger spiral

You are familiar now with the relationship between what we think and how we feel. A situation such as a rude boss may be the external trigger and our thought, 'How dare he speak to me like that?', triggers the emotion of anger. It is the thought that drives the emotion – at least initially. However, once in the spiral, the emotion then drives further negative thoughts, such as, 'He really is a bully. He shouldn't be allowed to get away with it.' In turn, this makes you even angrier than before, and so on, until the anger gets quite out of control. Where you lack the ability to manage your anger, this can create an extremely dangerous situation in many ways.

Have you recently found yourself in an anger spiral? Think about your emotions at the start of the situation, the middle, and the end of the situation. Did your anger increase in the way we have described above as your thinking became more negative? How long did it take for your anger to go down? Were you able to do anything positive to calm yourself?

Let's take a look at someone who gets into an anger spiral and learn from his mistakes. We'll use thought challenging as our tool to see how we can help our guinea pig reduce his angry thoughts and responses.

Our guinea pig

Neil is a 35-year-old computer specialist. He works in a high pressure job, feels stressed most of the time, and is perpetually offended at a myriad of slights and abuses. He is highly competitive and takes absolutely nothing lightly. In his mind, others are just out to annoy him, make his life difficult, and increase his stress – an indifferent shop assistant, a slow driver ahead of him, a leisurely bank clerk – any of these things can trigger his rage.

To help Neil, we're going to break his pattern of anger down into a series of steps. Each step represents a 'choice point'. Neil can choose to intervene at each step, cool down, and break the pattern, or he can continue along his destructive path.

Exercise 38

To help you learn how to get out of your own anger spiral, read Neil's difficulties and see if you can work out in advance what he could do to get out of his anger spiral – where his 'choice point' is (remember, these are choice points that you also always have – learn to identify them). What would you do if you were him, and what can you learn from what happens?

The 'should' rule

As we mentioned earlier, much of our anger is based on the premise that others 'should' think and act the way we do. They should share our values and behave as we believe that they 'should'. An important step in getting rid of angry emotions consists of breaking the 'should' rule.

Much of Neil's life is governed by such rules. He has rules and expectations for his own behaviour, for others' behaviour, and even feels the weight of others' rules on him. He has more rules than a legal tome. The result? Anger, guilt, and intense pressure to live up to his standards.

Yet Neil cannot live up to such unrelenting standards, and neither can others (and neither can you). Neil demands, 'People should listen to me.' 'They should stay out of the way.' 'I should have total control over this situation.' But the fact of the matter is that people don't listen, they do get in his way, and he cannot control their behaviour. At this point, Neil has the choice to accept the circumstances that have arisen or battle away against reality, demanding that it should not be that way. It would be much more preferable if he was listened to and left alone, but he cannot demand it.

Exercise 39

Neil has an option to challenge the 'should' style of thinking that is causing him to get so angry.

What could Neil say instead of the thoughts he has? Based on the work you have already done on the link between thoughts and emotions, write a short script for Neil. Then check below to see if you are thinking along the right lines.

For the first step, here are some anger reducing thoughts for Neil.

- 'The fact of the matter is that people do ignore my wishes and intrude. What, constructively, can I do when that happens?'
- 'I can continue to follow my own "rules", to treat others fairly and well, but not insist that they respond to me in the same way. It would be nice if they did, but if they don't, then they don't.'
- 'I need to stop disturbing myself about something I can do nothing about.'

Key point: Rigid thinking, with lots of 'shoulds' in it will ensure that we lose control of our emotions very quickly when others fail to respond to our rules. Learning to be more flexible in our views of how others behave will reduce anger and stress.

Exercise 40

This will help you banish your own 'shoulds'. Do you have 'should' rules for how others should behave? Write a few of them down. For example, 'People should not drop litter in the street'.

Now re-write these sentences without using the word 'should'. This may be quite hard to do for some of the rules in which you believe strongly. However, it will help you to begin to think more flexibly and to reduce the anger you feel when people ignore the rules that are important to you.

Coming to terms with the idea that others might not follow our own ideas about behaviour is a good start.

Some other tools to calm down angry situations

As the second step, work out what's *really* upsetting you. Examine what really hurts when one of your rules is broken. For example, when Neil is angry and hurt, he can ask himself, 'What really hurts here?' Maybe he thinks, 'People are rude and insensitive', 'I'll be made the victim', or 'I'm powerless to do anything about this.' What hurts the most is Neil's inability to change people's behaviour.

Exercise 41

What could Neil say instead of the thoughts he has above? As you did previously, write a short script for Neil. Then check your suggestions against ours below.

As the third step, here is how Neil might calm himself:

- 'There is no evidence that I should be able to control people.'
- 'People are responsible for their own beliefs, behaviours, attitudes and assumptions.'
- 'Perhaps I can see myself not as a victim, but as a person who can choose how to be.'

Neil can respond to hot, anger-driven thoughts with cooler, more level-headed thoughts.

- Neil initially thinks, 'How dare he?' but he can replace that thought with, 'He thinks he is trying to help me.'
- Neil thinks, 'How stupid can she be?' but he can instead respond, 'She's human.'

> **Key point:** To reduce your anger, change your script.

Exercise 42

This will help you change your script. Who or what annoyed you the most in the last couple of days? Recall how angry you felt, and what you were thinking.

Using any of the tools we've discussed so far in this chapter, change the script. How angry do you think these alternative thoughts would make you?

Using relaxation skills

The fourth step is to respond to angry feelings themselves. Neil can do this by practising relaxation and deep breathing. He can relax his muscles and refocus his attention away from the stressful situation. Learn to do this yourself. We touched on this briefly in Chapter 04, but now we are going to look at these skills in greater depth.

When your emotions take over, your body reacts by increasing your heart rate in order to move blood very quickly around the body. This, in turn, causes your breathing to become shallow and quick. To reduce your anger, your task is to reduce your heart rate and breathing to a point where your body is able to relax at will.

You can use breathing and muscle relaxation together for maximum effect. Try both, and see if either suits you better, or if a combination of the two is the most ideal.

Deep breathing

Learning to control your breathing is actually a big step towards controlling many of your 'high' emotions. Becoming physically relaxed calms down our brains, which prevents our emotional mind from dominating the proceedings. If you learn this simple skill, and practise it regularly, you will be well on the way to managing your anger.

Firstly, start noticing how you breathe.

- Find some space somewhere and lie on the floor on your back, with your knees slightly bent, in a relaxed position.
- Place your right hand on your stomach, just where your waistline is.

- Place your left hand in the centre of your chest.
- Now, without changing your natural rhythm, simply breathe in and out, and look out for the hand that rises highest when you breathe in – is it your right hand (on your stomach) or your left hand (on your chest)?

This will tell you, in simple terms, whether you are a deep breather (when the hand on your stomach lifts the highest) – or a shallow breather (when the hand on your chest rises higher). The chances are that if anger is a problem for you, you will be a naturally shallow breather.

Exercise 43

To help you check your breathing, take a little time out to become aware of your breathing when you are (a) in a stressful situation and (b) relaxing. Notice whether your breathing gets deeper or shallower, faster or slower. When in the day is your breathing at its absolute slowest?

Exercises to improve your breathing

You are seeking to 'feel' your breathing relax your body – and you will know when this happens. Many experts may tell you, 'Count to four', 'Count to six', 'Count to eight' when you breathe. This may be confusing and it can lead some people to hyperventilate. Instead, find a count that suits the length of your breath and within which you can feel a rhythm that is comfortable and breathing that is slow and deep. Whatever works for you is fine.

Horizontal or vertical? Another option, which you should decide for yourself, is whether you sit down or lie down. You can lie down if you prefer. However, bear in mind that the goal is for you to be able use this skill 'whenever and wherever', and so sitting, or even standing, will be a better option.

1 Place your hands on your stomach and chest, as you did before. (While this is good for practising, if you use deep breathing away from home or in a crisis situation, simply imagine this part.)
2 Now breathe in slowly through your nose (if you want to count to, say four, please do).
3 Ensure as you do this that the hand on your stomach rises, and the hand on your chest remains as unmoving as possible.

4 Now exhale slowly (count again if this helps you) and, as you do, feel the hand on your stomach gently fall back.

This is a simple breathing technique that you can use whenever you like.

> **Key point:** Learning to breathe well isn't difficult – but it is perhaps one of the most important skills you can use to reduce high emotion.

Muscle relaxation for calming emotion

A surprising, quick and easy calming trick is yawning. We tend to think yawning simply indicates tiredness or boredom, but on many occasions it is actually helping to calm us down. Yawning ensures more oxygen enters our lungs and moves into our bloodstream, de-tensing muscles and de-stressing our brains.

So if you feel a yawn coming on, and you have enough privacy, don't stifle it – use it as the ultra deep breath that it is and let it flow right through you.

The idea behind muscular relaxation is that it will eventually enable you to relax yourself quickly and at will, thus immediately helping to reduce anger and other high emotions before they become out of control. Progressive muscle relaxation involves tensing and relaxing, in succession, 16 different muscle groups of the body.

To begin, practise all of the exercises, and you will soon find that some seem to work for you better than others. If this is the case, select only those exercises to practise, and eventually reduce these to just one or two. You will have these exercises 'at the ready' when your emotions appear to need some extra management help.

Make sure you are in a setting that is quiet and comfortable. You can choose whether to sit in a chair or lie down – most exercises lend themselves equally well to either. Take a few slow, deep breaths before you start. Then tense each muscle group hard for about 10 seconds and let go of it suddenly, enjoying the sensation of limpness. Allow the relaxation to develop for at least 15–20 seconds before going on to the next group of muscles. Notice how the muscle group feels when relaxed, in contrast to how it felt when tensed, before going on to the next group of muscles. You might also say to yourself 'relax' as you do so. Here are the 16 exercises.

- Clench your fists. Hold for 10 seconds and then release for about 15–20 seconds.

- Tighten your biceps muscles by drawing your forearms up towards your shoulders and 'making a muscle' with both arms. Hold for about 10 seconds and then relax for 15–20 seconds.

- Tighten your triceps – the muscles on the undersides of your upper arms – by extending your arms out straight and locking your elbows. Hold, then relax.

- Tighten your forehead muscles by raising your eyebrows as high as you can. Hold for about 10 seconds and then relax for 15–20 seconds.

- Tighten your jaws by opening your mouth so widely that you stretch the muscles around the hinges of your jaw. Hold, then relax. Let your lips part and let your jaw hang loose.

- Tighten up the muscles around your eyes by clenching them tightly shut. Hold for about 10 seconds and then relax for 15–20 seconds. Imagine sensations of deep relaxation spreading all around the area of your eyes.

- Tighten the muscles in the back of your neck by gently pulling your head way back, as if you were going to touch your head to your back. Focus only on tensing the muscles in your neck. Hold for about 10 seconds and then relax for 15–20 seconds. Repeat this step if your neck feels especially tight.

- If you are lying down, take a few deep breaths and tune in to the weight of your head sinking into whatever surface it is resting on.

- Tighten your shoulders by raising them up as if you were going to touch your ears. Hold for about 10 seconds and then relax for 15–20 seconds.

- Tighten the muscles around your shoulder blades by pushing your shoulder blades back as if you were going to touch them together. Hold the tension in your shoulder blades for about 10 seconds, and then relax for 15–20 seconds. Repeat this step if your upper back feels especially tight.

- Tighten the muscles of your chest by taking a deep breath. Hold for up to 10 seconds and then release slowly. Imagine any excess tension flowing away with the exhalation.

- Tighten your stomach muscles by sucking your stomach in. Hold and then release. Imagine a wave of relaxation spreading through your abdomen.

- Tighten your lower back by arching it up. (You should omit this exercise if you have lower back pain.) Hold, then relax.

- Tighten your buttocks by pulling them together. Hold, then relax. Imagine the muscles in your hips going loose and limp.
- Squeeze the muscles of your thighs all the way down to your knees. You will probably have to tighten your hips along with your thighs, since the thigh muscles attach at the pelvis. Hold and then relax. Feel your thigh muscles smoothing out and relaxing completely.
- Tighten your feet by curling all of your toes downward. Hold, then relax.

Now imagine a wave of relaxation slowly spreading throughout your body, starting at your head and gradually penetrating every muscle group all the way down to your toes.

Key point: Regular practice will help you hone these skills until you can use them speedily and easily on any occasion.

Prevent stress and anger from making us act spitefully

As a fifth step to reducing his anger, Neil needs to look at how he gives himself permission to think in a thoroughly spiteful way. These thoughts allow Neil to treat others in ways that he himself would not want to be treated. 'He deserved it.' 'I just want her to hurt the way I have been hurt.' 'This is the only way I can get my point across.' Neil needs to recognize these ideas as con artistry. They con him into throwing aside his morals and engaging in threats, sarcasm and demands. Neil must remind himself of the costs of such strategies, and the benefits of remaining calm and fair.

Control aggressive behaviour

The sixth step is to look at the aggressive behaviour that comes from angry thinking. Neil gives himself permission to act aggressively and ignore the rights of other people. Imagine Neil getting worked up with a sales assistant who is interminably slow. He starts speaking loudly and rudely, and demanding to see the manager. The assistant then gets angry back and a row ensues. What other choices does Neil have?

- He could attempt to understand the cause of the assistant's slowness.
- He could put himself in the assistant's shoes, imagine what they are thinking and feeling, and attempt to understand their point of view.
- He could ask himself how important the delay really is.

This will help to:

- decrease Neil's anger
- decrease the assistant's anger
- increase the likelihood that the assistant will hear what Neil has to say
- increase the likelihood of Neil and the assistant having a rational and reasonable conversation.

Learning to own your anger

One of the difficulties of managing our emotions in difficult situations is the idea that none of this is our fault. If the other person had not done this, that or the other, we would never have reacted in that way. Actually, you may be partially right. Someone may have been extremely thoughtless, careless, acted stupidly or whatever, and you may be the victim of their rotten judgement. However, while the other person is responsible for their actions, you are equally responsible for your response.

- You are the owner of your anger.
- You are the decision maker and decide when and to what extent you use this emotion.
- No one else decides this for you.
- Of course, people sometimes work very hard to provoke you. Nonetheless, managing your anger in an emotionally intelligent way is still your responsibility. You control – and therefore decide on – your reactions.

> *Usually when people are sad, they don't do anything. They just cry over their condition. But when they get angry, they bring about change.*
>
> Malcolm X, political activist and speaker

Reducing angry emotions with humour

Using humour is an excellent tool for defusing anger. It can help you gain a more balanced perspective and help you find the funny side. For example, if you have spent the entire afternoon putting together a flat-pack bookcase, and as you stand back to admire it, it falls apart, you can either get furious or laugh. Try laughter. This will take a lot of the edge off your fury, and humour can always be relied on to help relax a tense situation.

Exercise 44

To help you use humour to defuse anger, use the following technique after you have felt angry about something. Relate the events that have made you angry during the day to a friend or partner. Only this time, you have to tell them as though the events are a funny story. Find something amusing about the fact that your scarf caught in the hedge as you were running for a bus, causing you to miss it. Make spilling coffee all over yourself unintentionally at work sound funny. This will get you into the habit of 'seeing the funny side' and you will gradually be able to do this 'in the moment', rather than becoming enraged, and only finding humour at a later stage.

Summary

- Of all the emotions we need to learn to manage in order to become truly emotionally intelligent, anger can be the hardest. It seems to gain a momentum of its own that leaves us feeling we are no longer in control of what is happening.

- We call losing control of our anger an 'anger spiral'. In this chapter, you have learned several ways to get out of this spiral and manage, reduce and eliminate your angry emotions.

- Remember what physical sensations high anger brings with it, and work hard on breathing and relaxing in order to control these. Look too to your cognitive, thought-challenging skills. Opinions are not facts. They are only what you think. Find different ways to think that will stop you getting so wound up.

- Own your anger. Many people do nothing about managing their anger because their view is that it is always caused by somebody else. This is quite untrue. No one else can make you angry. You decide whether to be angry or not.

- Become more open-minded and get rid of your 'shoulds'. The more rules you have about what others should and should not do, the more likely you are to become angry. Remind yourself that while it would be nice if others held the same values and ideas that you have, if they don't, that is fine as well. Your rules are yours to live by if you feel they have value, but it is not for you to decide what others' rules for living should be.

- Try to learn to see the funny side. It is hard to both laugh and be angry at the same time.

- Finally, do consider professional help if you are struggling. Anger management courses or one-to-one therapy assistance can really help, and the results will be life-changing (and perhaps life-prolonging).

  How much more grievous are the consequences of anger than the causes of it.

  Marcus Aurelius

part three

emotional intelligence and others

As you learned at the start of Part two, over and above the different competencies and ideals that come together as emotional intelligence (EI) is the larger umbrella of intra-personal and inter-personal skills. You will now have a much greater understanding of the intra-personal (self-awareness) skills that will bring you harmony in your life.

However, the quality of our relationships with those around us – friends, family and work colleagues, as well as the many strangers who regularly come into our lives in various guises – is defined by what is often called our 'people skills' or 'inter-personal skills', the level at which we relate to others.

This part of the book helps you to develop the skills of getting along with others and to develop 'other-awareness' – the ability to notice and understand what is happening around you, and to act upon what you see in an emotionally intelligent way. All the qualities and competences we look at in this part will help you to develop other-awareness. Linking other-awareness to self-awareness will give you all the skills you need to develop your emotionally intelligent self.

08

social responsibility

In this chapter you will learn:
- to begin using emotional intelligence in inter-personal relationships
- to understand the emotional intelligence skills involved
- to develop 'other-awareness' generally
- to identify the emotions of others which will enable you to connect with and respond to others in an emotionally intelligent way.

Developing empathy and understanding

> *[Empathy] means to sense the hurt or the pleasure of another as he senses it and to perceive the causes thereof as he perceives them, but without ever losing the recognition that it is as if I were hurt or pleased and so forth.*
>
> Carl Rogers, psychiatrist

Empathy is commonly defined as an ability to recognize, perceive and directly feel the emotion of another. It is often characterized as the ability to 'put oneself into another's shoes' or to experience the outlook or emotions of another within oneself.

Empathy is arguably the basic building block for positive relationships. It also encourages motivation. We are far more likely to act on someone else's behalf, to help them out and support them, if we can feel and appreciate their emotions.

Learning to understand someone else's point of view

We can never truly know what another person feels – and it would be impertinent to assume that we could – but in order to connect closely with others, we need to be able to appreciate at least something of their perspective. We can often achieve this in the simplest and most straightforward way by expressing to another person what we understand to be the emotions they are feeling. This allows the other person to feel heard and understood. You need never worry if you are wrong, as the other person can simply correct you with 'No, I wasn't quite feeling that, I was feeling this…' and this will help you to fully understand, rather than make an assumption that might be wrong.

Learning to develop empathy

The qualities of empathetic people are that:

- they have close, intimate relationships with others
- they are able to communicate clearly and openly with most people
- they have a genuine interest in the concerns and difficulties of other people

- they are able to appreciate someone else's point of view, even when they don't personally agree with it
- they are able to forgive without rancour.

Empathy is very powerful. Each time you use it to show understanding of a tense or antagonistic encounter, you shift the balance. An argumentative and difficult exchange becomes a more collaborative alliance. When you achieve this, you increase your ability to move to a satisfactory outcome for all concerned. No one, after all, is going to give you what you desire if they feel misunderstood or under attack. When you express an understanding of their position, they feel heard and understood. The emotional bond between you strengthens, and the other person is more inclined to work with you, not against you.

Misconceptions about empathy

Don't confuse empathy with sympathy. Sympathy – while a valid emotion – is more concerned with your personal view of events. It is an 'If I were you...' statement, suggesting that you would feel sorry for the other person's dilemma if you were in it. Empathy shows an understanding of the emotions that the other person might be feeling. Sympathy can sometimes be described as 'colluding' – 'Oh, how dreadful', 'Oh, poor you' – whereas empathy expresses an understanding of the other person's position even where you don't feel sympathy for it.

Empathy isn't agreeing or approving. It is acknowledging an understanding. You may totally disapprove of another person's actions, but you may also understand their own need to act in that particular way.

When empathy disappears

One of the hardest challenges of developing empathy is that it tends to fall by the wayside when we need it most. This is when emotional intelligence will come to your aid. When we are under stress, feeling misunderstood, irritated or on the defensive, we can easily let our emotions rule the day. We respond without thinking, and can appear insensitive or resentful.

This takes us back to the work we did on self-awareness in Part two. You can use this to gauge your emotions – your mounting irritation, for example – and contain your impulses and act sensibly in the face of provocation.

Using EI skills will enable you to call upon your empathetic side in order to understand the other person's position.

> **Key point:** Make it a rule always to express to another person what you perceive to be their point of view before you tell them your own and you will be developing empathy. In other words, let someone else feel heard and understood before you say, 'Now let me tell you how I view this.'

Exercise 45

To help you develop your empathy, for the next week practise being 'open-minded'. Empathy requires genuineness, and open-mindedness is the key to this genuineness. Whenever someone makes a statement that you strongly disagree with, rather than simply launching in with your alternative views, practise seeing their point of view by saying something like:

• 'That sounds like you think…'

Or:

• 'You obviously feel very strongly that…'

There is nothing wrong with disagreeing with someone, but being open-minded means that you don't invalidate their view – you have respect for it, and appreciate that the way you feel is only a point of view, as well.

Learning to take responsibility

> *Responsibility: a detachable burden easily shifted to the shoulders of God, Fate, Fortune, Luck or one's neighbour. In the days of astrology it was customary to unload it upon a star.*
>
> Ambrose Pierce, *The Devil's Dictionary*, 1911

Often, one of the most difficult things to do is to take responsibility for the mistakes we make in life, especially in relationships with others. This is because it is very hard to admit that we, and not the other person, are wrong or have handled things badly.

If we are really honest with ourselves, we know that we make these mistakes quite often. We end up hurting people we love, blaming others for our misfortunes, letting down people who have trusted us, and perhaps offering hollow apologies.

Learning to take better emotional responsibility means understanding why we keep repeating these errors, and taking steps to correct them. It does also, of course, mean accepting that we are fallible human beings, and that it is part of being human to sometimes get things wrong. This is also taking responsibility, but in a slightly different way. It is taking responsibility for the fact that we are not perfect, and that this is okay.

The games people play

Eric Berne, the founder of a therapeutic model called Transactional Analysis – popularized in such books as Wayne Dwyer's *I'm OK, You're OK* – very effectively explains why we make the emotional mistakes we do. In his book, *Games People Play*, Berne suggests that if you focus on the various conversational transactions that take place every day between people, you will notice some patterns. Some people become threatening to get what they want. Others turn someone's efforts at a serious conversation into a joke. Some people try very hard to make someone else feel guilty, or to present themselves as a victim. Berne notices that these conversations usually ended up with someone feeling emotionally distressed – sad, angry, controlled, frightened, etc. Berne refers to these errors as 'the games people play'. In contrast, conversations that go smoothly make people feel good. These conversations are free of games.

When we play emotional games, we tend to take on one of the following three roles:

1 rescuer
2 persecutor
3 victim.

Rescuers take care of people who should be taking care of themselves – taking responsibility for their well-being, arguing on their behalf, letting them off the hook, preventing them from making their own decisions or from finding their own way.

Persecutors tend to criticize, preach and punish. They want to verbally beat people into submission in order to get their own way or simply to prove they are superior.

Victims are generally incapable of making any decisions at all, letting others run their lives and take care of them. This becomes a downward spiral of dependency and victimhood. The less a person does, the less they are capable of, and the more they require other people to run their lives for them.

This isn't to say that, on occasion, adopting one of these roles isn't emotionally sensible. However, when we use them to manipulate a relationship, such roles become harmful and unproductive.

Exercise 46

Do you ever get involved in game playing? No? Be honest. Write down three instances you can recall in the last few months where you have tried to offload personal responsibility for something onto someone else. Then write beside it R (rescuer), P (persecutor) or V (victim), depending on which role you think you were taking in this game.

Key point: Where we don't take emotional responsibility, we not only damage relationships with others, but also our relationship with ourselves.

The habit of being proactive, or that habit of personal vision, means taking responsibility for our attitudes and actions.

Steven Covey, writer

Learning to take emotional responsibility

Taking emotional responsibility doesn't mean 'getting it right' all the time. We know enough now to understand that our emotional brain sometimes rides roughshod over reasonableness, and we often look back on a trail of emotional destruction. In the aftermath, our rational brain kicks back in, and we may thoroughly regret how we behaved. This is normal and natural – we are not suggesting that any of us become super-human beings who never put an emotional foot wrong.

Taking emotional responsibility asks only that we learn from our mistakes and attempt to fix emotional damage by making an effort to define and admit the faults and errors we have committed. The biggest problem is that very few people are emotionally skilled enough to apologize sincerely and non-defensively. In short, most people don't know how to say that they are sorry.

The art of apologizing

The thought of making a deeply felt apology strikes terror into the heart of the average person. They will consider an apology as 'losing face', backing off, allowing the other person to 'win', and they will consider it weak or humiliating. Yet the opposite is in fact true.

Key point: An emotionally intelligent person will be willing to admit mistakes and apologize for any harm caused by his or her actions.

Responsibility does not only lie with the leaders of our countries or with those who have been appointed or elected to do a particular job. It lies with each of us individually. Peace, for example, starts within each one of us. When we have inner peace, we can be at peace with those around us.

His Holiness the Dalai Lama

How to apologize

Even when understanding the principle, 'Sorry' can be the hardest word to say – especially when we don't really feel it. Taking emotional responsibility in a relationship doesn't mean taking the role of:

- victim – 'It was all my fault.'

Or:

- rescuer – 'It wasn't my fault, but I'll take the blame anyway to make you feel better.'

It means, very often, simply being the bigger person and being willing to be the one to own an error of judgement. Here are four steps to help you:

1 Be willing to admit to yourself that you have made a mistake. This can be a difficult starting point because it can mean accepting your own inadequacies – 'What an idiot I am.' 'Now look what I've done.' etc. However, as you go through the full process of taking emotional responsibility, these feelings will be replaced by those of confidence and well-being.

2 Be willing to admit your mistake to others. Not only are we beating ourselves up for making an error, but we are exposing ourselves to the wrath or disappointment of others! Learn to overcome this fear. You will discover that admitting mistakes is an empowering experience and a key factor in becoming an emotionally intelligent being. Others recognize the courage it takes to apologize and will usually think much better of you for having done so.

3 Convey genuine regret. You will need to develop empathy before you can convey genuine regret. This is not just about saying sorry, it is about expressing a genuine understanding of how the other person may be feeling due to what has happened. Only when another person feels that you really understand their view will your apology feel genuine to them, and be genuine to you.

4 Put things right when you can. Taking responsibility for a mistake usually means making amends of some sort. How to achieve this may not be obvious, and you don't need to have all the answers. The simple question 'How can I put this right?' or 'Is there any way that I can make amends?' is making amends in itself. You don't have to offer a solution. Asking someone to suggest what you can do is just as effective, possibly more so, and it suggests a willingness to put things right 'their way' rather than 'your way'. Making amends must, in any event, be something you and the person you are apologizing to decide between you, so that you achieve a mutually positive outcome.

> **Key point:** You may find that one of the hardest parts of becoming emotionally intelligent is owning up to the mistakes you have made in your relationship. But this is a crucial step, so please don't attempt to avoid it.

Developing forgiveness

Forgiveness is almost a selfish act because of the immense benefits it offers to the one who forgives.
                                        Lawana Blackwell, writer

An inability to forgive will damage, or bring to an end, many personal and work-based relationships. How often do we hear someone say, 'I will never forgive her for that' or 'I will never get over what he did to me'? Nonetheless, forgiveness is not easy, especially when we feel that we have been grievously harmed, and we often hold on to the grudge and let it eat away at us over a period of years, if not a lifetime.

However, forgiveness is worthy of negotiation. Where we have been badly hurt emotionally, we do have the right to express to the person who has hurt us that our forgiveness may be dependent on their being willing to understand the pain they have caused. It is much easier for us to forgive harm that someone has done to us if they are willing to acknowledge the harm they have done. However, this is not always possible and then we are faced with a decision to make.

By being unwilling to forgive, are we able to get on happily with our lives, or are we filling our lives with bitterness and anger that cannot be overcome by anyone other than ourselves? In other words, where our lack of forgiveness causes continuing heartache, are we continuing to harm ourselves?

Father Harold Kushner in *The Sunflower: On the Possibilities and Limits of Forgiveness* (1997, pp.185–6) gives an excellent example that may place this in perspective.

> *A woman in my congregation came to see me. She was a single mother, divorced, working to support herself and her three young children. She said to me, 'Since my husband walked out on us, every month is a struggle to pay our bills. I have had to tell my children that we have no money to go out, while he is living it up with his new wife in another part of the country. How can you tell me to forgive him?' I answered her, 'I'm not asking you to forgive him because what he did was acceptable. It wasn't. It was mean and selfish. I'm asking you to forgive because he doesn't deserve the power to live in your head and turn you into a bitter, angry woman. I'd like to see him out of your life emotionally as completely as he is out of it physically, but you keep holding on to him. You're not hurting him by holding on to that resentment, but you're hurting yourself. Forgiveness happens inside us. It represents a letting go of the sense of grievance, and perhaps most importantly, a letting go of the role of victim.'*

> **Key point:** Kushner's example shows us that forgiveness isn't a weakness, it's a strength. It is not a condoning of wrong-doing, but a desire to let go of grievance and move on.

My fault or theirs?

Bear in mind that many grievances we harbour in personal relationships are subjective. In other words, we see a person's behaviour one way – they see it another.

> **Key point:** Being willing to let go can be extremely empowering when we are able to say, 'Okay, that's not how I see it, but let's move on anyway.'

The emotionally intelligent value of compassion

If you want others to be happy, practise compassion. If you want to be happy, practise compassion.

His Holiness the Dalai Lama

Compassion for others is essential to EI, but stirring up compassion in ourselves is not always easy.

Is compassion different from empathy? It essentially arises through empathy, and it could perhaps be called 'empathy in action'. It is using empathy – an understanding of someone's plight – in a practical way by offering some kind of physical or emotional support. In other words, compassion is an emotion that embraces a sense of shared suffering, most often combined with a desire to alleviate or reduce the suffering of someone else as if it were one's own.

Many years ago, compassion was described to me as 'the ability to feel your pain in my heart'. I have always felt this definition would be hard to better.

Compassion differs from other forms of helpful or humane behaviour in that it focuses primarily on the alleviation of suffering. In this way it is different to altruism, which is where kindness is more likely to confer a benefit than to relieve suffering – 'Here, have my last doughnut'. The difference may be marginal, but it's there.

Exercise 47

The EI skill of other-awareness will assist you to develop compassion. Look around you. Be more aware of the lives of others. Every day, life gives us innumerable chances to open our hearts, if we can only take them. An old woman passes you with a sad and lonely face and two heavy bags full of shopping she can hardly carry. Stop for a moment and absorb what you see and become aware of your emotions. (You may even decide to help her with her shopping – active compassion.) Switch on a television, and see on the news a mother in a war-torn country kneeling above the body of her murdered son, or an old grandmother in a developing country trying to sip the thin soup that is her only food.

In the moment you feel compassion within you, don't brush it aside or shrug it off and try quickly to return to 'normal'. Don't be afraid of your feeling or be embarrassed by it, and don't allow yourself to be distracted from it. Use that quick, bright rush of compassion – focus on it, develop it, enhance and deepen it.

Is there anything you feel that you might like to do to actively change the life of someone else for the better – even in the smallest way? This is the beginning of empathy in action.

> *To care for anyone else enough to make their problems one's own, is ever the beginning of one's real ethical development.*
>
> Felix Adler, writer

It is hard to expose yourself to the plights of others, but actively doing so, and then identifying your emotions, will develop your compassionate nature and enable you to connect more closely with those close to you, who form part of your own life.

Learning to become non-judgemental

> *My desire is to be a forgiving, non-judgmental person.*
> Janine Turner, actress

Increasing emotional intelligence by decreasing judgement

Being judgemental is such a subtle characteristic that most of us do not realize that we have it. It seems completely natural to us to develop views on anything and everything – which is perfectly healthy, of course – and we do not realize that we can slip into what is called 'negative bias' when relating to others.

There are two problems associated with harbouring judgemental views of others:

1 We become narrow thinkers ourselves. We decide that because we think something, that makes it a fact. We can also become naturally critical – instead of noticing someone's nice hairstyle, we focus on their inappropriate footwear. This negative bias prevents us from relating to people positively and cheerfully.

2 We fail to connect with others in a warm and empathetic way. If others feel that we may be critical of them, they will probably avoid us or adopt a defensive stance when talking to us.

Judgemental people try to foist their beliefs, their habits and their way of life on others. They are critical of people who don't see life the way they do. 'But my way feels right,' you may say. Well, your way feels right to you because of who you are, and it *is* right for you. Yet it is arrogant to think that others should always see things in the same way that you do. For all of our differences, as long as we aren't causing harm and havoc, we deserve love, respect and acceptance. The antidote to being judgemental is to become open-minded.

Learn to achieve open-mindedness

In the same way that a person who misuses alcohol may need to stop drinking totally, your own way forward is to stop judging – totally. You must stop evaluating others as being good or bad, right or wrong.

This will require a great deal of willpower and commitment, but the rewards will be enormous. As you stop judging others, you stop judging yourself. You will see that we cannot quantify good or bad, right or wrong. Our views are almost always subjective, and learning acceptance of them will be quite empowering.

Exercise 48

To help you become less judgemental, for the next week (at least) do the following:

- Give up moral judgements on the behaviour of others. This will be hard, especially in some circumstances. Tell yourself that others are making what they see to be the best choice of behaviour available according to their own needs and values at the time.

- When you read newspapers or watch television news programmes, stop yourself from automatically making an instant 'right or wrong' judgement.

- Stop rating others as being better or worse than anyone else. Simply accept people as unique individuals.

- Stop using critical descriptions, such as 'selfish', 'stupid', 'ugly', 'lazy', etc.

- Select someone you know that you don't especially like. Consider what aspects specifically you dislike, and now try to reframe them in your mind in a non-judgemental way. When you next have contact with this person, practise being pleasant and non-judgemental towards them. Be aware of how they treat you in return, and how you feel afterwards.

Summary

This chapter has focused on what we call 'other-awareness'. In its simplest form, other-awareness involves no more than looking around you. Think of the person who stops suddenly in front of you in the street and starts rummaging in their purse or pockets, and gets out a street map or whatever. You stand behind fuming, as you cannot get by. Or consider the car in front of you whose driver stops to have a conversation with a friend he has noticed on the pavement. Or the shop assistant who keeps chatting to her colleague about their night out when you are waiting to pay for your purchase. Small irritations, but they leave you angry and frustrated.

- What makes you cross is people's lack of other-awareness – their self-absorption prevents them from noticing the needs and rights of others.

- Emotionally intelligent other-awareness must, necessarily, take active forms. It requires you to see not only the obvious, as in the above examples, but to search for the not-so-visible: consider that the friend confined to bed may not have someone to food shop for her; wonder whether a recently bereaved relative would appreciate your support; notice a work colleague struggling over work and offer assistance. In other words, it means not only considering the needs of others, but being able to spot those needs and then possessing the qualities needed to be able to help in a genuine way.

- We have looked at the competencies that will develop emotionally intelligent relationships with others such as empathy, forgiveness and compassion. Return to these again and again. Consider to what degree you already possess these qualities, and work hard on enhancing those you feel you need to.

In Chapter 09, we continue to look at relating to others, showing you how to develop your communicating and negotiating skills.

09

developing communication skills

In this chapter you will learn:
- to develop your listening skills
- to understand the importance of body language in communication
- to use assertiveness as a way to avoid conflict
- to achieve outcomes to negotiations with which everyone feels happy.

The importance of emotionally intelligent communication

Your ability to negotiate, communicate, influence, and persuade others to do things is absolutely indispensable to everything you accomplish in life. The most effective men and women in every area are those who can quite competently organize the cooperation and assistance of other people toward the accomplishment of important goals and objectives.

Brian Tracy, author

Communication is the most important skill in life. We spend most of our waking hours communicating. If you wish to attend, there is a myriad of courses you can sign up for on effective communication skills that cover public speaking, presentation giving – anything where you have to stand up and speak to get your message across. This is important of course – you need people to understand you and your message. But what about listening? What about understanding what others have to say? Try and find a course on listening rather than speaking and you will be hard pressed. Listening is not highly regarded as a skill we should develop. Yet it is the most essential part of effective communication, of developing deep and meaningful personal and work-based relationships, of simply understanding people and their viewpoints.

Communicating well and listening actively is a key component of emotional intelligence. 'Other-awareness' isn't simply observing and appreciating, it requires a strong ability to both express yourself clearly and to attend to and understand others fully.

> **Key point:** As a rule of thumb, when anyone speaks to an audience, they are likely to hear about 10 per cent of what is actually said. This sums it up – most people either don't listen, or they pretend to listen, or they listen only selectively.

Think about the reasons we need to communicate:

- to pass on information
- to ask for what we want
- to share how we feel

- to understand how others feel
- to achieve goals and outcomes.

If we learn to communicate well, we are more likely to achieve successful outcomes in any given situation, which equals being emotionally intelligent.

How to learn the art of skilled listening

A good listener is not only popular everywhere, but after a while he gets to know something.

Wilson Mizner (American author)

In his book 'How to Turn People into Gold', American author Kenneth Goode says 'Stop a minute to contrast your keen interest in your own affairs with your mild concern about anything else. Realize then, that everybody else in the world feels exactly the same way! Then, along with Lincoln and Roosevelt, you will have grasped the only solid foundation for interpersonal relationships; namely, that success in dealing with people depends on a sympathetic grasp of the other person's viewpoint.'

The skills you must practise

To improve your communication skills, work through those listed below and ask yourself whether you already use them. If not, start now.

Be actively present

Most people, when they listen, are not actively present with the other person. Most people are either talking, or they are simply waiting for the other person to finish speaking so that they can speak again. When we don't listen effectively we:

- annoy those who are giving us their time
- fail to hear vital information being given
- fail to grasp the other person's point of view
- lose ground in negotiating well
- weaken relationships.

Exercise 49

Some common listening weaknesses include the following. Place a cross next to any you consider apply to you:

☐ Getting distracted by thoughts that are nothing to do with what the other person is talking about.

☐ Interrupting and breaking the other person's train of thought.

☐ Making meaningless comments, such as 'Oh, I'm sure it will all work out right in the end.'

☐ Minimizing what is being said – 'Oh, I wouldn't get too upset about that if I were you.'

☐ Starting to show restlessness if the other person takes a while to tell their story.

☐ Agreeing too quickly with statements, simply to get the conversation moved on.

☐ Cutting in and giving advice, rather than letting the other person work through their thought processes.

☐ Stopping listening and spending your time planning what you will say as soon as you get a chance to speak.

☐ Actively attempting to drive the conversation in a particular direction – perhaps directing it to your own problems rather than the speaker's.

If you have more than one or two crosses, then you need to work much harder on your listening skills.

Active listening is actually a concentrated activity. We use a large range of skills to encourage the other person to speak and to make them feel comfortable.

Pay total attention

You cannot truly listen to anyone and do anything else at the same time.

M. Scott Peck (writer)

Show your interest by stopping all other activities. If the conversation is important, do everything you can to ensure that you will not be interrupted unnecessarily – close the door, suspend phone calls, tell others that you do not wish to be interrupted – and turn off your mobile phone.

Keep eye contact

It is vital that, when someone is speaking to you, you look directly at them. It conveys interest and respect – whereas constantly looking away conveys the opposite. This does not mean staring intently at someone, which can of course be exceedingly uncomfortable for both of you. It means maintaining appropriate eye contact, and looking away only briefly, from time to time.

Show positive responses

Responses can be both verbal and nonverbal (nods, hand movements, facially expressing interest) but however you do it, you must show that you received the message – and more importantly, show that it had an impact on you.

Even out the cadence of your voice

Speak at roughly the same energy level as the other person – then they'll know they really got through and don't have to keep repeating themselves.

Show understanding

To say 'I understand' is not enough. People need some sort of evidence that you have truly understood. Prove your understanding by occasionally summarizing the basis of their idea ('It sounds as though you really do want to go for that promotion') or by asking a question that proves you have grasped the main idea ('So if you decide to do this, what sort of timescale are you thinking of?'). The important point is not to repeat what they've said to prove you were listening, but to show you understand the point and purpose of what they are telling you.

It is the province of knowledge to speak and it is the privilege of wisdom to listen.

Oliver Wendell Holmes (writer)

Respect others views

Show that you take the views of others seriously. It seldom helps to tell people 'I appreciate your position' or 'I know how you feel', although don't dismiss these comments out of hand – they can be useful if you really are uncertain what to say, and if silence would be awkward. However, you really want to show respect by communicating with others at their level of understanding and attitude. You can do this by adjusting your tone of voice, rate of speech and choice of words to show that you are trying to empathize with the speaker's position.

Listening to and acknowledging other people may seem deceptively simple, but doing it well, particularly when disagreements arise, takes true talent. As with any skill, listening well takes plenty of practice.

Make sure not just that you understand, but that others feel understood

The greatest compliment that was ever paid me was when one asked me what I thought, and attended to my answer.
Henry David Thoreau (writer)

We usually feel most heard when someone reflects back to us what we have just said. For example, 'It sounds as though you are really struggling at present. Tom's away a great deal and with three children under five, it is often too much to cope with on your own.' The relief of being able to say, 'Yes, that's exactly how it is.' And knowing that you have been listened to and understood creates great respect and closeness between two people.

This is not an easy skill to master, and it does not come naturally to most people without a great deal of practise.

Key point: How you listen is very important. By listening in a way that demonstrates understanding and respect, you can develop rapport, and that is the true foundation from which you can relate well to others.

Exercise 50

Here are two examples of conversations where you have alternative responses. Decide for yourself which response reflects the speaker's viewpoint, and which the listener's.

1 **Speaker:** *My boss has laid off my assistant at work, and I really don't know how I am going to manage without her.*

Response A: Oh dear. That's just what you need right now, on top of all the other problems you have.

> **Response B:** I'm sorry about that. It sounds as though you are going to find things more difficult now that you have no one to help you.

2 **Speaker:** *I'm concerned about my relationship. Bill is behaving very distantly just now, and I'm not sure what's wrong.*

> **Response A:** Tell me about it! Jim does this to me all the time. I don't think there's anything wrong. It's just the way men are sometimes.

> **Response B:** I'm sorry to hear about that. It must be difficult not knowing why Bill is being distant right now.

What we are looking at here is the difference between responses that are:

a) focused on the speaker, or
b) self-centred.

A criticism of reflected responding is that it simply repeats what the speaker has been saying. However, there is a very good reason for doing this – it lets the other person continue with their own train of thought. You may yourself have experienced situations where you start to tell someone something that is important to you, but never get to finish what you wish to say as the listener has either asked a question that has taken the conversation off in another direction, or they have told you about a similar experience of their own. None of this is the end of the world – and of course we all do it from time to time. But where a person has something serious to say, reflective listening is an important and emotionally intelligent way of ensuring that that person has the opportunity and the space to speak and be heard.

Learn the value of summarizing

Summarizing is an important skill to ensure that you and the person you are talking to are still having the same conversation! Never merely assume that you have got the gist of what is being said – summarize what you believe you have heard. It is also important as, on occasions, we all tell our stories in over-long and rambling ways, with various side turnings and cul-de-sacs that may, or may not, be important to the central theme. Your summary is therefore like a précis of what has gone before.

How you can do this

You can start a summary, which should only be one or two sentences long, with phrases such as:

- Let me just be sure I have understood that. You're …
- OK. It sounds as though what's happened is …
- Tell me if I'm wrong, but I think you're saying that …
- If I've understood correctly, there's …

Summarizing has three great pluses:

- Like reflecting, it ensures that the speaker feels heard.
- It ensures that you haven't got the wrong end of the stick.
- It gives the speaker an opportunity to correct you if you have, or add further information to give clarity.

Body language – understanding the non-verbal messages you give out

'It's not what you say, it's the way that you say it' is a famous line, and we all understand what it means. Non-verbal messages are an essential component of communication. Most people assume that what we have to say is communicated mainly via what comes out of our mouths. Have a guess at the following:

Write down, in percentage terms, how much of our communication is via

- The words we say _____
- Our tone of voice _____
- Our body language _____

What have you put?

Here is the answer:

The words we utter account for roughly 10 per cent of our communication. Our tone of voice for 25 per cent, and our body language a staggering 65 per cent. Before you dismiss this, consider a couple of examples.

> You walk into a restaurant with a friend. As you sit down, you see a couple across the room. You cannot hear a word they are saying, but you notice some gesticulations and an angry look on the face of one of the diners, whilst the other one looks away and makes no eye contact. What would you assume is going on? Very likely, some sort of argument. But you didn't hear a word.

Picture the same scenario, but this time, the couple are leaning towards each other, their eye contact is obvious, and they are smiling. Now make another assumption. This time, I suspect you will guess that they are deeply connected, and possibly in a loving relationship. You still haven't heard a word.

Now flashback to your childhood. Earlier in the day you were working on a project in the dining room that involved scissors and glue, and you have a rather nasty feeling that some of the glue may have found its way on to the surface of the highly polished dining table. You have decided to say nothing and hope that it won't be noticed. Now you are upstairs in your room, and your mother is downstairs. You hear your name called. Just your name. Nothing else. You will almost certainly be able to tell immediately from the tone of your mother's voice whether (a) she is alerting you to the fact that your favourite TV programme is on, or (b) she has found the glue adhered to the dining table. Again, no words have been uttered, other than your name. In this case, tone of voice was the giveaway.

Most of us are more expert in reading body language than we realize, as the above examples may have shown. We can usually pick up whether someone is happy or sad, tense or relaxed. However, there are of course, two aspects to our Non-Verbal Communications (NVC):

- our ability to read the messages that others are giving us
- the messages we give out.

Many of us are less expert at assessing the messages that we give others, yet this is an enormously important part of social interaction. Here is a common conversation:

Mary: I've been telling you about my day and you are obviously not at all interested.

Jane: No, really, I'm hugely interested.

Mary: Well, you don't look interested at all!

Jane's NVC had obviously given her away! Think about the different characteristics of NVC that might enable you to become a more accurate giver and receiver of non-verbal messages. For example:

- Eye contact
- Facial expressions

- Gestures
- Posture and body orientation
- Proximity
- Humour.

Using your eyes

We have already spoken about the importance of good eye contact. Don't overlook this. When you make eye contact you open the flow of communication and convey interest, concern, warmth and credibility.

Smiling

Smile! Smiling is a powerful cue that transmits:

- Happiness
- Friendliness
- Warmth
- Liking
- Affiliation.

If you smile frequently you will be perceived as more likable, friendly, warm and approachable. Smiling is often contagious and others will react positively to you.

Gestures

Some of us can gesture quite a lot when we are speaking. We wave our hands and use specific facial expressions, nod our heads, etc. It makes what we say come alive. If you fail to gesture while speaking, you may be perceived as boring, stiff and unanimated. Gestures will make you appear more animated, as well as indicate that you are listening.

Standing tall

The way you walk, talk, stand and sit tells other people a great deal. Standing in a relaxed way and leaning slightly forward communicates that you are approachable, receptive and friendly. A feeling of closeness results when you and another person face each other. Speaking with your back turned or looking at the floor or ceiling is – very obviously! – going to communicate disinterest.

Don't get too close

We need to have an awareness of invading someone's space – simply getting too close to them physically. Sometimes we lean towards people who are speaking softly, but that can be perceived as over-closeness. It is better to be open, and invite them to 'speak up'.

Mirroring

Matching your body language to the speaker will help to give you further rapport. If they lean forward, do the same. If they lower the tone of their voice, adjust yours as well. This is especially useful if you are having a difficult conversation with someone. Using matching, or mirroring, works extremely well in keeping things calm and you are more likely to reach a satisfactory conclusion to the topic under discussion. Try it and see.

> **Key point:** Never underestimate the power of NVC when relating to others. You can communicate intimately and positively with someone on an emotional level without saying a word.

Becoming more assertive

Sometimes, the conversations we have are not easy. They are not about us happily listening to someone else recounting the details of their Italian holiday – or even seeking our advice with their problems. In those dialogues we are either in neutral mode or in control of the conversation.

What about difficult conversations, where we need every skill we possess not to allow things to descend into a disagreement? What you say, and how you say it, will decide whether you achieve a good (emotionally intelligent) outcome or feel stressed and upset when the conversation ends.

What is your personal style? Do you tend to be:

- passive ('Oh, all right then.')
- aggressive ('Because I say so, that's why.')
- assertive ('I'd like to help, but I'm too busy right now.')?

Unless you are already naturally assertive, developing this communication style will help you to defuse difficult conversations and remain emotionally in touch with the person you are having difficulties with.

The features of an assertive style

An assertive communication style means that you are:

- keen to find a solution to problems where everyone is happy
- strong enough to stand up calmly for your own rights
- able to accept without rancour that others have rights too
- interested in the other person's point of view.

Two major reasons for choosing to negotiate assertively are:

1 It is usually *effective*. Quite simply, you are more likely to get the outcome you want.
2 It is the style that *others appreciate the most*. Therefore, they are less likely to avoid negotiating with you because they can rely on you remaining calm and looking for a good outcome for both of you.

The basic difference between being assertive and being aggressive is how our words and behaviour affect the rights and well being of others.

Sharon Bower, author

Your emotional rights

A major feature of assertiveness is that you do have the right to say how you feel. The passive person fails to say how they feel, and the aggressor will not own their feelings, but will suggest that you 'made' them feel that way. Being assertive means saying 'I feel very unhappy when you speak to me like that' as opposed to 'You make me very unhappy when you speak to me like that'. This may seem like a finely tuned play on words, but it is actually emphasizing an important difference. You are taking responsibility for how you feel but, at the same time, explaining that their actions are creating these feelings in you.

Stand your ground

Staying calm and standing firm at the same time takes a lot of practice, but is well worth the effort. In order to do this, you need to keep things simple, and operate on a three-step basis.

Here is a sample situation:

Jenny's teenage daughter Donna wants to go to a pop concert and stay overnight with her boyfriend. Jenny isn't at all happy about this request. However, rather than simply saying 'no' (and at the very least causing resentment, or at worst, a big row), Jenny does the following:

1 She acknowledges Donna's request and feeling:

'I appreciate how important and exciting this would be for you, and how much you must be looking forward to it'.

2 Then Jenny states her own reservations.

'However, I am concerned for you staying overnight as you are only 14, so I am going to say "no" to that.'

3 Finally, Jenny offers a solution.

'Still, I know you really want to go to the concert, so why don't we arrange for a cab to bring you home which will give you the time to have a drink and a chat afterwards, before leaving?'

Notice the three steps:

1 Acknowledge.
2 Use 'but' or 'however' to state how you feel.
3 Offer an alternative solution where you can.

The 'Broken Record' technique

Of course, the situation above is in an ideal world of instant compliance. In the real world, Donna would be saying, 'Oh, but Mum...' and continuing to argue her case. In that case, you use the 'Broken Record' technique, which is exactly as it sounds. No matter how Donna pleads, Jenny keeps repeating her terms. She consistently acknowledges what Donna is saying: 'I am sorry that you are so disappointed with my decision.' 'I appreciate how cross you are that I am not going along with this.' Then Jenny will repeat her 'But' or 'However' and restate steps 2 and 3.

If you use this skill well, sooner or later, the other person will accept your terms and you will both feel happy with the outcome (the average 'come back' before the other person concedes is two to three times, so you can afford to wait it out).

Standing your ground can be done in a calm and understanding way that means you do not need to 'give way' and yet the other person will feel that they have achieved a result.

We are only briefly touching on the various skills that will help you develop your assertiveness. You may wish to read further books devoted entirely to this topic as the more you learn, the better equipped you will become to handle situations in a positive way and achieve a good outcome.

Key point: Becoming assertive means knowing how to express your views and opinions in ways that are not critical of, or offensive to, others.

Exercise 51

A good way to practise assertiveness skills is to role play. Perhaps you have a friend, partner or work colleague who might do this with you. You need your partner to be as difficult as possible while you practise the techniques we have outlined above. Then let them use the same skills on you. You will have fun and, if you can, ask them to agree to practise this regularly until you both feel confident enough to use the skills in 'live' situations.

Keeping an eye on the outcome

Achieving a 'Win:Win' result

Steven Covey, in his book *Seven Habits of Highly Effective People*, coins a phrase that has since become popular when negotiating. He calls it a 'Win:Win situation'. He identifies four possible outcomes to negotiations:

1 You win/they lose.
2 They win/you lose.
3 You both lose (no deal).
4 You both win.

Until Covey flagged up the pluses of win:win, most people thought of 'winning' in a verbal negotiation as meaning that the other person lost. An emotionally intelligent, elegant solution to a controversy, however, needs an outcome that everyone feels is fair. This requires many EI qualities and skills being used in abundance in order to keep a negotiation on the table until all the options have been explored and the most suitable one agreed on. This might well (and often does) mean compromise.

Nonetheless, where this is equal, or where one person gives one thing in order to gain another, compromise is very definitely win:win.

Yet sometimes the ideal of win:win does not happen, and Covey adds a corollary to this with 'Win:Win/No Deal' as the full negotiating tool. In other words, win/lose or lose/win are not emotionally intelligent options. Either you negotiate to the happy agreement of both parties, or you put it all aside for another day.

While there is not enough space in this book to detail the negotiating skills that might take you to this outcome, the principle is clear, and you should always keep it in your mind. However you get there, win:win is a good solution to all problems, so make it your goal at all times.

Summary

In this chapter, we have focused on how to use verbal and non-verbal communication skills to get along with others.

- 'Getting along' means not just listening (although that seems hard enough for many of us) but also understanding what is being said, and being able to express that understanding to the person speaking. It means having greater awareness of others' points of view, and appreciating that our own is just that – a point of view, not a fact or a truth.

- You have learned that good communication is not about bringing someone round to your point of view, but finding common ground – a point at which you can both say, 'Yes, I am comfortable here.'

- Not all conversations are easy. Many involve difficult negotiations or conflict resolution, and using EI to achieve this makes a good outcome more likely. Learning a little about being assertive in such situations – calm but firm – and practising this regularly will also ensure good outcomes.

- The idea of 'Win:Win/No Deal' is one that you can carry with you and use as appropriate. In most cases, remember that 'I win/you lose' is not a favoured outcome when keeping a good ongoing relationship intact is also important.

- Perhaps the most important skill of all is getting used to the idea of hearing, and understanding, what someone else has to say before contributing your own view. This is a stylish and effective way of communicating – but for most people it is one they are unfamiliar with. Work hard on this; it is one of the most important and emotionally intelligent communication skills you will ever master.

part four

four

emotional intelligence

in action

This part of the book involves taking the EI skills that you have been learning, and applying them to specific life circumstances where they may be especially helpful to you. Everyone has areas in their lives where things are going well, and perhaps some that are going less well than we would like. By looking at applying EI specifically to each one of these areas, we can give you specific opportunities to actively use your EI skills as you come to the end of the book.

10

emotional intelligence in the workplace

In this chapter you will learn:
- why emotional intelligence in the workplace is becoming important
- the emotional intelligence competencies required for workplace success
- as manager or employer, how to develop emotional intelligence skills in your staff.

It's tough out there

Changing values in the workplace

People who rise to the top of their field of business aren't just good at their jobs. They're affable, resilient and optimistic. In other words, it takes more than traditional cognitive intelligence to be successful at work, it also takes emotional intelligence – the ability to restrain negative feelings, such as anger and self-doubt, and instead focus on positive ones, such as confidence and congeniality.

Not only do bosses and corporate leaders demand high amounts of EI of others, and need it themselves, but every people-oriented job demands it too. A plus here is that, whereas IQ is relatively fixed, EI can be built and learned. The demand for EI is happening because the market place is tougher than ever and changing fast. This is due, in part, to:

- enormous advances in information and communication technology (ICT)
- increasingly global markets
- the rise of the internet
- an increase in the numbers of people now accessing professional education
- a more multinational workforce as mobility of labour becomes both easier and desirable.

New ways of working

This new contract of employment is a two-way trade. Employers have higher demands of their staff, but the employee makes higher professional development demands of their employer. Most jobs are no longer 'for life', but are often short-, fixed-term contracts of employment. Employees will often exchange this new lack of security for an agreement that they will be trained and developed not only in technical expertise but in the 'soft skills' that are now regarded as necessary for success. In short, they want to be in an environment where they can develop their EI.

> *Interpersonal communication and other so-called soft skills are what corporate recruiters crave most but find most elusive in MBA graduates. The major business schools produce graduates with analytical horsepower and solid command of the basics – finance, marketing and*

strategy. But soft skills such as communication, leadership and a team mentality sometimes receive cursory treatment.

Wall Street Journal, May 2000

Companies can test and teach EI, but while some employers are beginning to do so, many are not. These soft skills are often required, yet it is currently, in the main, left to the employee to identify their needs and weaknesses, and take whatever self-development route they can find.

This will change, but for the moment, developing your own EI competencies and learning to apply them in the workplace will be a better route to emotionally intelligent success than hoping your employer will develop these with you – other than through giving you situations in which you can practise them.

Key point: As the demands of employment change, and competition to achieve more and succeed better continues in this competitive marketplace, I cannot impress on you enough the value of developing your EI skills and ensuring that they serve you well in the workplace.

The emotionally intelligent employer and employee

An employer or employee with high emotional intelligence can:

- manage their own emotions
- communicate effectively with others
- manage change well
- solve problems quickly and well
- use humour to build rapport and understanding in tense situations.

These employers or employees will also:

- possess open-minded understanding
- remain optimistic even in the face of adversity
- be good at teaching and persuading in a sales situation and resolving customer complaints in a customer service role.

This clarity of thinking and composure in stressful and chaotic situations is what separates top performers from weak performers in the workplace.

Emotional intelligence competencies for workplace success

David Caruso and Peter Salovey (*The Emotionally Intelligent Manager*, 2004) identify four critical emotional skills that will develop an emotionally intelligent employee. You will be familiar with these from Chapter 01 but to summarize they are to:

- read people (identifying emotions)
- get in the mood (using emotions)
- predict the emotional future (understanding emotions)
- do it with feeling (managing emotions).

> *I found that for jobs of all kinds, emotional competencies were twice as prevalent among distinguishing competencies as were technical skills and purely cognitive abilities combined. In general the higher a position in an organization, the more EI mattered: for individuals in leadership positions, 85 per cent of their competencies were in the EI domain.*
>
> Daniel Goleman, psychologist and writer

Below I list the EI competencies that have been proven to contribute more to workplace achievement than technical skills, IQ and standard personality traits combined. They are well worth absorbing.

You have spent time throughout this book mastering these skills. I would like you now to understand how these skills can fit into your workplace environment and help you to develop your career more successfully, or to simply enjoy the level of employment you are at right now. I have therefore given you, for each EI competency, a list of reasons for the importance of ensuring that you either have, or develop, these competencies in your place of work (or to enable you to move on to a better place of work). Review them all, and make notes on areas that you can develop and work on.

Social competencies

How we get along with others at work.

Empathy

Our awareness of others' feelings, needs and concerns. This is important in the workplace because:

- empathy enables you to understand others better; it gives you a sense of others' feelings and way of seeing things, and it shows an active interest in their concerns and interests
- in these days of customer service being all important, the ability to meet customers' needs through understanding them is vital
- empathy increases your ability to understand what your colleagues need in order to develop and master their own strengths
- empathy enables you to embrace diversity of all types within the workplace more easily.

Good inter-personal skills

Good inter-personal skills assist us in achieving desirable responses in others. These are important in the workplace:

- to help you to use the most effective tactics and techniques to achieve desired results
- to give or to send clear messages that are understood by others
- to enhance your leadership abilities within your workplace
- to help you understand and participate positively in workplace changes
- to help you resolve disagreements with both clients and colleagues
- to create good relationships with customers, in order to achieve better business outcomes for all parties
- to enable you to be a good team worker, who gets along with others in the group.

Personal competencies

Self-awareness

Self-awareness is understanding yourself, your strengths and weaknesses, your values and principles – and how you can use them with EI. Self-awareness is important in the workplace for:

- recognizing your emotions and how they affect those around you
- knowing your strengths and also the present limits of your capabilities
- having confidence about your self-worth and strengths.

Self-management

This means managing your emotions, thoughts and responses. It is important in the workplace because:

- it assists your self-control – your ability to manage any disruptive emotions and impulses that might have a negative effect in the workplace
- it engenders trustworthiness, and helps you to maintain standards of honesty and integrity that will be respected by others
- you will be willing to take personal responsibility and be accountable for your personal performance
- it helps you to remain flexible in the face of unexpected changes
- it helps you to absorb and embrace new ideas.

Self-motivation

We talked about this in Chapter 05, and it is crucial in the workplace in order to ensure that you reach important goals and targets. Self-motivation in the workplace:

- encourages you to strive to meet and improve your own standard of excellence
- encourages you to commit yourself fully to your organization
- encourages you to use your initiative – to be proactive rather than reactive to situations
- develops persistence in the face of adversity.

Exercise 52

To help you develop your EI in your place of work, take time to consider the above. Now make a list of EI competencies that you think would benefit you in your own particular workplace, and identify specifically when these competencies might be of use.

Rate these competencies on a scale:

1 = I find this quite easy to use

10 = I find it extremely hard to act with EI in these situations.

Start practising with the easier ones (lower rated) first. As you become more confident, start practising those you find more difficult – referring back to the relevant sections of this book for renewed guidance. For example:

EI competency	When it would be relevant	I have used this successfully...
Self-control	During weekly sales meetings	Last week: my targets were down due to circumstances outside my control. Instead of being upset by the criticism, I prepared ahead of time and calmly presented my rationale, which was well received.

Work through your own list in the same way.

Becoming a good team leader

Organisations need emotionally intelligent managers who will help to develop the competencies and commitment to work together in the new knowledge economy.

Pat Fritts, organizational consultant

In the modern workplace, the idea of 'manager as coach' is becoming commonplace. The changing shape of organizations means that we require a new style of management that can help to develop soft skill competencies as well as technical capability.

How you can achieve this

If you find yourself in this management role, you will need to manage the development of your staff in EI terms by:

- encouraging the development of their emotional capabilities
- helping them to resolve differences using a win:win EI style
- developing their problem-solving skills using EI, rather than 'battery ram' skills
- teaching them to communicate effectively by developing their listening and understanding skills
- increasing their personal motivation through encouraging goal setting aimed at their personal, as well as professional development. (Employers are interested in employees' personal development now almost as much as their professional development when they look for well-rounded team members.)

In order to activate these aims, you have at your disposal the skills and techniques in this book that you can organize into a series of development tools for your staff.

Developing yourself through developing others

When you are coaching and developing others, you will also be continuing to develop your own EI competencies. As a summary to help you, these are the skills you will need to use:

- your active listening skills
- your reflecting, summarizing and questioning skills in order to encourage meaningful discussion and open responding
- your ability to negotiate and encourage, to challenge and find solutions
- your ability to set goals, so that you can encourage staff members to do the same
- your ability to work on mutually agreed strategies for success
- your willingness to encourage your staff members to discover and follow up other learning resources.

You will also need to demonstrate your own EI behaviours:

- to show empathy
- to be non-judgemental
- to find the positive, rather than the negative
- to be willing to evaluate your own EI skills
- to demonstrate integrity
- to show tact and diplomacy
- to use humour appropriately.

Your emotional intelligence employee appraisal

Coaching in 'soft skills' requires offering your staff comprehensive feedback similar to that which you would give for an employee's technical abilities. You will therefore need to bring all of this together into a workable and measurable written framework for your employee(s), which should include:

- a realistic appraisal of the goal the employee is aiming for
- an assessment of where the employee is now
- a goal plan – how to get there
- regular feedback regarding results achieved
- possible re-evaluation of goals set.

Summary

It is now well established and accepted by the majority of businesses that EI, not simply technical expertise or education, is exceedingly important in defining excellence in the workplace. This chapter has given you a taste of how you might transfer the EI skills you are developing to your place of work.

- If you are an employee, you will find increased success in your career through emotionally intelligent strategies in the workplace.

- If you are a manager/employer then you will need to use EI yourself and find ways to develop these EI competencies in your staff. Don't simply demonstrate EI yourself; actively set up internal programmes designed to train and develop people in these skills. They will appreciate the training, and your company will prosper.

> *The rules for work are changing. We're being judged by a new yardstick: not just by how smart we are, or by our training and expertise, but also by how well we handle ourselves and each other. This yardstick is increasingly applied in choosing who will be hired and who will not, who will be let go and who retained, who passed over and who promoted.*
>
> Daniel Goleman,
> *Working with Emotional Intelligence*

emotional intelligence within an intimate relationship

In this chapter you will learn:
- the emotional intelligence qualities you need to ensure a good personal relationship
- how to best deal with the conflicts that arise in most relationships
- how to use love and understanding to keep your relationship on track
- how to overcome jealousy
- how to part (if it comes to that) with dignity.

175
emotional intelligence within
an intimate relationship
11

Inside the heart of each and every one of us there is a longing to be understood by someone who really cares. When a person is understood, he or she can put up with almost anything in the world.

Reverend Edward Hird

Emotional intelligence and romance

The best test of how a person uses their emotional intelligence may be in their romantic relationships. In romance, feelings are strong and personal, and it is easy to feel hurt, rejected or disappointed. Within any relationship that contains emotion, intellectual intelligence alone will not be enough. Romantic relationships work best when each person has a high level of EI as well as other appealing qualities.

Your emotionally intelligent resources for good personal relationships

You now have a great many EI competencies to work on, but there are some that apply a little more strongly than others in the area of intimate, emotional relationships. To be emotionally intelligent within a personal relationship of importance, you need to be:

- self-aware
- capable of empathy
- not over-impulsive
- generous and kind, with a positive outlook
- persistent and willing to hold on to your dreams and hopes.

Exercise 53

To help you assess these EI skills within yourself, ask yourself the following question:

'Do I possess and practise EI in my most intimate relationship(s) or do I operate on a completely different, emotionally driven basis – reserving my EI skills for friends, family and work colleagues?'

Be honest. Now think about the EI skills you are familiar with, and consider how you could better apply them to this significant relationship.

Gender differences

Do EI qualities apply to both sexes equally? Well, yes and no. John Gray's seminal book *Men are from Mars, Women are from Venus* indicated that men and women do operate differently. This is not to say that men don't share the same emotions as women, but that their emotions are slower to come to the fore. Men may think in practical terms first, whereas a woman's emotions can sometimes kick in quickly and strongly. Gray's book was important in allowing men and women to understand these basic differences about each other, and to make allowances for them rather than become frustrated by them.

Mary and John Valentis, in *Romantic Intelligence: How to be as Smart in Love as you are in Life*, (2003), identify a few EI qualities that do differ slightly for women and men, as follows.

Emotionally intelligent woman	Emotionally intelligent man
Emotionally straightforward	Has a strong sense of responsibility for his behaviour
Cool and unflappable	Has the courage to face his feelings
Can make a commitment	Can commit to his partner and his ideals
Has a healthy ego but is not self-involved	Is sympathetic and caring
Is sensual and open-minded about sex	

To be honest, I'm not sure how many of us could consistently live up to all of these listed EI qualities! However, the idea is to have an awareness of them and how they lead to the key components of EI in an intimate relationship.

The emotional intelligence skills you need for intimacy

Emotional self-awareness

The joy of this is that it has nothing whatsoever to do with being perfect (the ideal most of us feel we *must* strive for in order to retain the interest of our partner). It has everything to do with knowing ourselves – simply identifying and being in tune with our feelings, whatever they are, even if they change from moment to moment.

Recognizing patterns of behaviour

One of the values of identifying emotions is to help you recognize patterns of behaviour. For example, if similar problems occur again and again, you will have similar emotions. By identifying the emotions precisely, you will see the behaviour patterns faster than if you simply try to compare one situation to another. This is your brain doing a good job for you. Your mind naturally makes comparisons between similar situations, so you are facilitating the process. Where you see a pattern emerging in experiencing the same emotions, either within one relationship or within each relationship you have, it may be an indication that you have some work to do on managing your emotions and your emotional needs.

Benjamin Disraeli once defined madness as, 'Doing the same old thing again and again, and expecting different results.' Do bear this in mind.

Encouraging emotional compatibility

Kindness in words creates confidence. Kindness in thinking creates profoundness. Kindness in giving creates love.

Lao Tzu, philosopher

Emotional compatibility is the most significant predictor of relationship success. This means, ideally, that you and your partner possess similar levels of EI in order to share similar levels of trust, intimacy and an ability to express emotions.

It is something that we all long for, but what constitutes emotional compatibility exactly? How can we work on achieving it if we feel the levels of it are presently low? The answer is by taking responsibility in a relationship.

Emotional compatibility starts with the premise that your happiness and fulfilment begin with you, not with your partner. You are ultimately responsible for your own happiness, and if your partner feels the same way, your compatibility levels will be high. If you don't feel that is particularly the case at present, then use your EI skills to make the changes you need. In other words, by changing yourself, you will provide a catalyst for change for your partner, since he or she will then respond quite differently to you. Here are some EI suggestions for you to work on:

- Take more responsibility for your own emotions.
- Learn to explain your emotions without blaming your partner for them (use 'I feel...' rather than 'You make me feel...'). Take responsibility for your own insecurities, defensiveness and unmet emotional needs. These may have been around for a long time and have little to do with your present relationship. Find ways of dealing with these things that don't involve your partner.
- Learn to manage your own negative emotions. Don't rely on your partner to do this for you. The more you can do this, the more you will be able to help your partner in a positive way.
- Ask yourself questions such as 'How do I want to feel?' and 'What can *I* do that would help me feel better?' – rather than thinking in terms of what your partner can do for you.
- Take this further. Ask yourself 'How would my partner like to feel?' and 'What can I do to help him/her feel that way?'
- Be confident and open in telling your partner what you need from them. However, learn to change your demands into preferences – 'I would prefer...' rather than 'I want...' – and don't place too many demands on your partner.
- Remember that sometimes, even when you express your feelings responsibly and own them, you can trigger feelings of defensiveness from your partner if they misinterpret what you say as personal criticism – even when this was not your intent. Be aware of this, and take responsibility for addressing it with your partner, so that you can both take a look at where there was a lack of clarity. Use your EI listening skills. In particular, listen for the emotions behind the words. This is very hard to do when you feel that you are being attacked, but that may be when it is most needed.
- There is a difference between caring about how someone feels and feeling responsible for how they are feeling or for making them feel better. This means being empathetic, but not a rescuer. It is more developmentally helpful for your partner to learn to take personal responsibility in just the same way that you are doing.
- Don't give too much information – and pick your timing. Sometimes, although full disclosure is the ideal, it can be better to keep your feelings to yourself, or share them at a

more appropriate time when you are both relaxed and available to listen to each other.

- Above all, don't depend on your partner for your happiness. If you do you will start to need them rather more than love them. Where need takes priority over love, your compatibility levels will drop. Remember that happiness should be something you bring into a relationship more than something you get out of it.

Using emotional intelligence when things go wrong

Your relationship may be solid and compatible, but still occasionally suffer from upsets and disagreements. This is normal, as I am sure you know. Love is never about not disagreeing – it is about how to deal with disagreements in an emotionally intelligent way and find solutions that work well for both of you. To achieve this, you need to *take joint responsibility*.

> *You come to love not by finding the perfect person, but by seeing an imperfect person perfectly.*
>
> Sam Keen

Problems within relationships are not the sole responsibility of one person, and sharing problems and solving them together can be an extremely strong relationship-builder. There is a myriad of reasons why problems can arise. These problems may be practical (money worries, illness, work difficulties) or they may be more emotionally based and involve you and your partner simply not seeing eye to eye on things that are important to each of you.

By taking joint responsibility for problem solving, you are behaving in an emotionally intelligent way. Doing this is not always straightforward. Your partner may see the problem as entirely yours – or vice versa. So you may initially need to use the negotiating skills you learned in Chapter 09 in order to reach an agreement on this.

> **Key point:** Remember, you are not asking your partner to take joint responsibility for the problem. You are asking them to take joint responsibility for finding a solution. Making this distinction is vital for mutual understanding.

What are the keys to resolving difficulties? Of course, with any dialogue, irrespective of the content, you will need to draw on your EI skills of *empathetic listening and responding*.

The listening skills you have already developed, or are working on, become hugely valuable within an intimate relationship. Revisit Chapter 09 if you need to review these skills. There is always so much more emotion in intimate personal relationships and consequently a few further points need to be considered that would be less relevant with other relationships.

1 Stick to the concern of the moment. Don't rake over old ground or widen the disagreement.

2 Consistently use the word 'we' when looking for resolution, rather than 'I' or 'you'. 'How can we resolve this?' is a much better approach than 'What are you going to do about it?' This is a vital ingredient in cementing a team approach to problem solving and will make a real difference.

3 Your goal is to be on the same side of the fence with regard to your problem. Keep this in mind at all times and avoid the boxing match approach of attack and defence.

4 Never forget the saying 'You cannot win an argument'. (If you are uncertain as to what this means, refer back to Steven Covey's 'Win:Win' analogy when negotiating – look back at Chapter 09.)

5 Never generalize the specific. If someone has burned the sausages, say just that, don't say 'You're a lousy cook'.

6 Do not use threats or allow your language to become too vitriolic. Consider the impact on your partner. How would you feel? Will it help? Never stop checking these things with yourself.

7 Think consistently about outcomes and results. 'Will speaking or acting this way get me what I want, or will it simply alienate my partner?'

With the best of intentions, we all sometimes become over-emotional, anger bursts through and we lose track of what we are saying or trying to achieve. When this happens, simply take a break. Don't berate either yourself or your partner for losing control. That's life. We're fallible human beings. The only important question is: 'Where do we go from here?'

Be the bigger person

Never shirk from apologizing. It is the best calmer of troubled waters there is. Don't consider it a weakness; it is a strength. It is being the bigger person.

An apology opens the gates for further discussion, usually in a more mutually respectful way. Failure to apologize may mean the issue is never resolved. Not only are resentments harboured, but there is a much bigger consequence – you have failed to learn how to resolve a difference, and this will not bode well for future differences of opinion.

> **Key point:** Remember, you are not apologizing for whatever the disagreement was about – that is a dialogue to return to. You are apologizing for your emotionally unintelligent behaviour and for losing control. This requires courage and will gain you a great deal of respect.

> **Exercise 54**
>
> Learn from experience.
>
> If EI goes out of the window and unhelpful emotions take over, and you do not feel that you can resurrect the discussion with your partner, take the time to reflect and ask yourself the question, 'What have I learned from this that will make me better able to gain a successful outcome next time?' Make a written note of the points that occur to you. You may even decide to share these with your partner on some future occasion. You won't be bringing up the old row, but you will be bringing up the thoughts you had about your own emotions and behaviours in the midst of it, and offering possible solutions for doing better next time.

Develop emotional honesty

Always be emotionally honest with each other. This is different to being factually honest (although this is also essential, of course). It means telling each other how you really feel. If you are uncomfortable with something, or concerned or afraid, try to say it honestly. Instead of saying 'You shouldn't do so-and-so' or 'I don't want you to do so-and-so', say 'I am afraid if you do so-and-so, so-and-so will happen'.

Overcoming jealousy

A mistake many people make is to believe that jealousy is an indication of how much we love somebody. In fact, it has nothing to do with love. It is purely about low self-esteem and lack of confidence.

Sadly, this very destructive emotion is often a self-fulfilling prophecy. I have worked with many clients who became so jealous of not knowing exactly what their partner was doing when he or she was not with them that they became excessive in their demands and suspicions. The problem with this is two-fold. Not only are you likely to drive your partner away but, worse, you despise your own behaviour, which lowers your self-esteem even more. You then believe that you are not worthy of being loved by your partner and that they will no doubt now be looking for someone else – and the possessiveness gets worse not better.

Accept risk

An emotionally intelligent relationship must accept an element of risk or you will stifle your partner. You must also bring an element of realism into your relationship. There will be times when your partner will prefer to be with someone other than you. This does not mean that he/she is going to leave you. This is a fact of life that you must come to terms with and accept.

Insuring against risk

Think of being able to purchase an insurance policy that would guarantee you complete faithfulness from your partner in absolutely all circumstances. A discreet private eye will follow them around the whole time. You will know where they are every minute, and you will know that, even when you hear that they are talking to someone else, you will never have a moment's worry. Would you like to purchase that? You bet!

However, the cost of this policy is a million pounds. Still interested? No, I thought not. The point of this is that the cost is too great. The guarantees that you are looking for just aren't realistic. Have the confidence to live with the risk that is almost certainly only in your head. Work on your self-esteem. This is the culprit, not your partner.

Look back to Chapter 06 on resilience. Save your energies for if or when something does actually happen and deal with it then. Worrying now will only sabotage a good relationship that would probably have endured.

How to cope when a relationship ends

Relationships end for many, many reasons. Within the scope of this book I offer one small piece of advice that will make a very large difference. Where possible, when a relationship ends – even when your heart is broken – *act with dignity if you can*. The clients I work with who find it hard to deal with their emotions and move on are often more wracked with guilt at their own poor behaviour at the end than at losing the person they loved. Inelegant behaviour will compound your pain.

This advice is easy to give and hard to take but please, do bear it in mind. If you can bring emotionally intelligent emotions and behaviour to bear even in the face of great personal pain, you will be stronger for it, and recover better.

Summary

In this chapter we have looked at the key factors necessary for your relationship to flourish in an emotionally intelligent way, as well as how to deal with conflict, jealousy and the worst-case scenario of your relationship ending.

- Use what you have learned, not just in this chapter, but throughout this book, to think in terms of what will enable your own relationship – either one you are part of now, or hope to be part of in the future – to flourish.

- Never move away from the principle that romantically intelligent love is one that brings out the best in you and your partner. It allows room for you both to grow, to develop, both as individuals and together. It enables you to live life passionately and be fulfilled.

- While you may both constantly evolve and change, your ability to remain consistently open with each other about your feelings, to be able to understand and respond to the emotions of the other person, and to consistently draw on the qualities that engender trust and understanding are what will create an emotionally intelligent quality to your love that will be enduring and, hopefully, unwavering.

  The secret of a happy relationship is not finding the right person. It is being *the right person.*

  Anon

12

developing emotionally intelligent children

In this chapter you will learn:
- how to encourage your own children to develop emotional intelligence
- how important your own behaviour is in your child's emotional development
- how to teach your children to develop confidence, resilience and respect for others.

Family life is our first school for emotional learning.
Daniel Goleman, psychologist and writer

NB: To avoid the use of 'he/she' throughout the text of this chapter, your child will sometimes be referred to as he, and sometimes as she.

Just as you have wanted to learn more about emotional intelligence yourself, and how you can develop it, you need to use similar skills to develop EI in your children. It is much easier to learn the skills of EI as a child, and they will become set and enduring by the time your child reaches adulthood.

How to begin

The first step in fostering EI in your children is to make a fundamental shift in your view of parenting. Many parents see their role as someone who attempts to mould their child according to their own preconceived ideals. Not only can this be ineffective, it can actually increase a child's sense of rebellion when they consider that they see things quite differently to the way you do.

A more emotionally intelligent way of parenting is to help your children become more at ease with their own emotions and with their families. This type of parenting recognizes that your children will have emotional experiences almost every day of their lives and encourages you to help them learn how to manage these emotions – and to model this behaviour yourself.

It's very difficult to see your children being sad or angry. But when you brush aside their feelings with a 'Cheer up!' or 'Don't speak like that', you are making it more difficult for your children to be able to identify and deal with those feelings. In other words, you lower their emotional intelligence.

So how do you go about it?

While for parents, EI means being aware of your children's feelings, and being able to empathize, soothe, and guide them, for children – who learn most of their lessons about emotions from their parents – it includes the ability to control impulses, wait for what they want (delayed gratification), motivate themselves, learn social skills and cope with life's ups and downs without a fuss.

Parents who get involved with their children's feelings are rather like emotional coaches. Like sports coaches (which they often are, as well), they teach their children strategies to deal with life's ups and downs. They don't object to their children's displays of anger, sadness or fear and nor do they ignore them. Instead, they encourage their children to learn more about emotions, and to express them appropriately, rather than inappropriately. They also teach their children to understand and respond positively to emotion in others. The bonus of teaching children these important life lessons is that the parents build closer relationships with them.

> *Grown-ups never understand anything for themselves, and it is tiresome for children to be always and forever explaining things to them.*
>
> Saint-Exupéry, *The Little Prince*, 1943

Learning the basic steps

Teaching EI to your children requires you, the parent, to work on five basic steps. You will not find these steps difficult at this stage as the concepts will now be familiar to you.

1 Become aware of your child's emotions (in just the same way as you have learned to become aware of your own).
2 Recognize these emotions as an opportunity for intimate discussion.
3 Listen empathetically, and don't diminish your child's feelings.
4 Help your child find words to label the emotions he is experiencing.
5 Explore with your child ways to solve the problem at hand, rather than simply telling her not to be so emotional.

What difference is all this hard work going to make?

If you consistently practise these steps, your children will have the opportunity for:

- better physical health
- doing better academically than children whose parents don't offer such guidance
- getting along better with their friends
- having fewer behaviour problems
- being less prone to temper tantrums and/or acts of violence.

In general, it has been found that children who are encouraged to develop an understanding of their emotions experience fewer negative feelings and more positive feelings. In short, they're emotionally intelligent.

Also, when you use this style of parenting, your children become more resilient. Of course, they still get sad, angry or scared under difficult circumstances, but they are better able to soothe themselves, bounce back from distress, and carry on with productive activities. In other words, again, they are more emotionally intelligent.

Case study

It was a warm summer's afternoon, and eight-year-old Johnny and his younger brother Sam, age six, were playing out in the garden. Living in a loving environment with financial security, the boys had access to most of the current and trendy outdoor toys from bikes to ride to mini assault courses to climb. For a while they played contentedly, until Sam started banging around with a wooden spoon against a tin bucket that had been set out to catch rainwater. As is the way with young children, despite the plethora of toys and games available to him, Johnny decided that what Sam had was what he wanted to play with. He went over to Sam and asked him if he could 'have a go'. Sam, realizing that he was in possession of something his brother really wanted, of course said 'No'. Johnny started shouting, 'Let me, let me', to which Sam responded by whacking Johnny's leg with the spoon and continuing his game. Johnny became furious. Screaming at Sam, he flung himself on him and a noisy fight ensued – at which point, the boys' father appeared and, after a struggle, managed to physically separate them.

He asked the boys to explain what had happened. They both spoke at once, crying, accusing and blaming the other for 'starting it' and telling each other 'I hate you'. Their father asked them to stop for a moment and to each take five deep breaths. The boys attempted this, gulping back sobs as they did so, but it calmed them down. Their father than waited a moment, before saying to them both, 'It sounds as though you have both got very angry over this.' The boys agreed eagerly, glaring at each other. 'Okay,' said their father, 'Johnny, did it really upset you when Sam wouldn't let you share his game?' 'Yes,' said Johnny. 'And Sam,' said Dad, 'How did you feel when Johnny wanted to play this game instead of you?' 'I felt that it wasn't fair,' said Sam. 'Johnny had all the other toys and I only wanted this one.' 'Okay,' said Dad, 'So you felt it was unfair of Johnny to want your toy, and Johnny felt upset with you that you wouldn't let him play.' The boys agreed. 'So what's the solution, do you think?' asked Dad. Johnny spoke first, 'Well, I would like to play this game, but I guess I can wait a bit. We can tell the time quite well, so I could show Sam my watch and we can agree for ten minutes each, perhaps. In fact, perhaps we can do that with other things as well. We do often argue about who has what.' 'But who will go first?' asked Sam. 'What do you think?' asked Dad. 'Well, perhaps we should take turns at that,' said Sam. 'That would work,' said Johnny.

'Okay,' said Dad. 'What great solutions you have come up with. Now, is there any last thing you want to say to each other before you both come in and have an ice cream break?' 'Sorry Sam.' 'Sorry Johnny,' quietly chorused the boys.

Johnny and Sam were shown by their father how to turn around a potentially explosive situation, and not only to get along with each other but to find solutions they could use again and again to prevent future emotional uprisings.

Let's explore how to teach basic, essential skills that all children need, such as being able to let go of upsetting experiences or take in positive ones.

Your child's emotional well-being will be greatly increased by using some, or all, of the exercises below on a regular basis. For children, who usually delight in routine, this should be relatively easy, and these exercises will soon be second nature to them.

Exercise 55

Help your child to relax. This is something that parents rarely think about with a child. Children bounce around, full of energy, with their reactions more a matter of the body than the mind. However, it is worth parents appreciating that, when their child's body is more settled, their reactions usually become calmer and it is easier for them to think clearly, to control themselves, and to remember what has been said.

This is why knowing how to settle a child's body down is extremely useful to a child.

One of the best ways to teach this skill is at night, when your child is already more relaxed and open and more willing to try (or put up with!) some new things just to keep you in the room. We suggest trying out some of these techniques with your child and find the ones that work for him. As with most things, the easiest way of teaching these skills to your child will be to make everything into a game that is funny and interesting. This way they will constantly want to 'Do it again!'

- Draw letters or shapes on his back and see if he can work out what they are. Even a two-year-old can recognize a circle or a square. (My two-year-old grandson absolutely loves this and is always asking for 'More, more!'.)
- Get him to screw up his muscles for about five seconds and then relax completely. You will need to show him how to do this, and you can make it fun by getting him to screw up his face and his hands to start with, which he will find both easy and funny – especially when he sees the funny faces you make doing the same thing!
- Teach him to take big breaths. A good trick for teaching this is to get your child to breathe out fully and then hold the exhalation for a couple of seconds. When he inhales, he'll naturally take a big breath in (which he will also, no doubt, find very funny).
- Suggest he imagines that he is very heavy, sinking more and more deeply into his bed. If you try this yourself, you will realize that this is a wonderful relaxation technique that you may decide to keep up with for yourself, or at least do alongside your child.

You only need to spend a few minutes a night on these relaxing exercises, and you do not need to undertake all of them. You will both decide your favourites very quickly, and of course, you will want to choose the one your child is clamouring for!

As your child gains more experience, you can ask her to relax her body increasingly on her own, especially if she is old enough to understand more of what this is about. During the day, you can gently encourage your child to recall those feelings of relaxation and to use the techniques she has learned.

Exercise 56

Help your child to let go of upsetting feelings. In exactly the same way as happens with adults (see Chapter 02), upsetting experiences are stored in your child's emotional memory. If a similar situation occurs, these memories are activated and intensify her reactions. So teaching her how to filter out painful feelings at the end of the day or as the day goes along can be very helpful. Again, at night, when you've got a captive audience, you can follow the relaxation by asking your child to recall anything that was upsetting during the day, and then get her to release those feelings through one or more of the following.

- Let her vent her feelings for a few minutes. During that time, try not to dampen her feelings (for example, by saying 'Oh, it's not as bad as all that.').
- Suggest that she exhales the feelings with each breath. Perhaps imagine that the breath is like a broom that sweeps dusty feelings away: good riddance!
- Get her to imagine her feelings draining out of her body, perhaps as if there were tiny openings at the tips of each of her fingers and toes.
- Suggest she imagines her feelings being swept away by standing in a rushing stream on a beautiful, sunny day, or putting the feelings into a jar and tossing them into the sea from a sailing boat.
- At the same time, encourage her to say to things such as, 'I'm letting my sad/painful/cross feelings go', 'It's all right' or 'I feel better now'.

As with relaxation, encourage your child to use these methods increasingly on her own, both at night and during the day.

Encourage your child to focus on the good things

A child has a lot of positive experiences in a day, but many may not be especially noticed or absorbed. Yet if the good moments sink in, they become a source of soothing and encouragement that he can draw on the next time things get difficult. This is teaching him to focus on the positive, and will help him to counter any negative thoughts he might have. Being able to recall good experiences helps to balance against the painful moments of life in his emotional memory.

*One of the virtues of being very young is that you don't
let the facts get in the way of your imagination.*

Sam Levenson, author

For example, paying special attention to good experiences can
give an anxious child the sense of being loved and safe that he
really needs. Equally, it enables a spirited child – zooming
around so much that new experiences are constantly crowding
out old ones before they have a chance to register – to become
more aware of positive experiences in general.

Exercise 57

You can teach your child how to make good moments a part of his
nightly routine as well, after you have helped him relax and let go
of any distressing feelings. As with those skills, encourage him to
use what he's learning on his own, both in the evening with you in
the room, and during the day by himself.

Simply take a little time to look back over the day and talk about
the nice moments within it, such as pleasant moments with you,
learning a new skill or any praise from others. Focus especially on
any events that are the opposite of how your child might normally
feel about something. For example, if he is a little nervous around
animals, talk with him about petting a dog and recalling that it was
really good fun when the dog licked his hand.

It's important that he does not just recall a nice event but that he
experiences a nice feeling, so ask him if he can remember how he
felt at the time, and allow him to enjoy reliving those pleasurable
emotions.

Promoting resilience in your child

None of us want our children to have to learn to deal with
painful and difficult situations from experience if we can find
another way to prepare them. Using visualization will help you
do this.

Exercise 58

Suggest to your child that she picture a difficult situation and then,
while remaining completely relaxed, get her to see herself dealing
positively with this. Start with relatively easy situations (perhaps
finding something to eat on her dinner plate that she didn't want)
and work up to more challenging ones as the days go by (perhaps
a difficulty at school).

For example, you could ask a cautious child to imagine being accidentally bumped into while standing in line at school, and encourage her to see herself remaining relaxed and calm and not worried about it. Or you might ask a more spirited child to imagine another child beating her at a computer or board game and then to picture herself not getting upset by it, but staying relaxed and calm and telling herself she'll probably win next time.

Encourage your child to imagine the positive outcomes that would result and the good feelings she would have.

If children grew up according to early indications, we should have nothing but geniuses.
Johann Wolfgang von Goethe, writer

Imagination – a child's best (imaginary) friend

Exercise 59

This is a nice, three-step exercise that you can practise with your child, in order for him to use his imagination about desired outcomes.

- Ask him to imagine a situation where he sees himself acting in an effective, positive way. An example might be sharing a chocolate bar with a friend who had forgotten to bring one for school break. Then encourage him to imagine how good that would feel.
- Next, ask him to imagine the same situation, but this time seeing himself acting in a more selfish way – keeping the chocolate bar for himself, perhaps – and then invite him to imagine the possible bad outcome (his friend calls him selfish, or goes off with someone else) and the sort of feelings he might feel (sadness or guilt, for example).
- Finally, ask your child to choose which way he would prefer to act, now that he has identified how he felt on each occasion (this will hopefully be the more positive, generous approach). You can also ask your child to explain to you what this teaches him about feelings and actions that he will be able to carry forward with him for the future.

Help your children control their thoughts and feelings

Bearing in mind that so many adults don't seem to manage it, the idea of being able to teach a young child to have control over his thoughts, feelings and behaviours might seem something of a tall order. However, even young children can be taught these skills. By adjusting your approach to the age of your child, there are many ways in which you can do this.

Exercise 60

Encourage your child to begin to recognize when she is getting, for example, anxious or angry. You can help by asking relevant questions, such as, 'How upset are you feeling at the moment – a little, medium or a lot?' You can then ask your child, 'What is going through your mind, as you feel this way?' This gives her the chance to make the connection between what she is thinking and how she is feeling. Once she has identified the thought (perhaps, 'I think it is unfair that John got a bigger part in the form play than I did.'), you can help your child begin to argue with these negative thoughts. As usual, you start by doing it for her – 'Well, you got into the football team and John didn't,' or 'John's part may be bigger, but your part is more interesting.' Then encourage her, over time, to do this type of thinking more and more on her own.

A good, fun way to move in that direction is for you and your child to take turns in coming up with a reason why some negative thought is wrong. Have a competition to see who can come up with the most. For example, if she is worried about burglars, you could help her come up with this list of reasons why she's safe:

- The doors are locked. (you)
- The lights are on. (her)
- No one has ever been burgled in our street. (you)
- Three dogs live next door that bark at anything that moves, and burglars stay away from dogs like that. (her)

Hopefully, you will now have many new ideas for developing EI in your child or children. The nice thing is that you work at this together so you will possibly develop a much closer relationship with your child than otherwise. You will learn with each other and from each other.

Here are a few more ideas to think about that will bring everything together.

- Your children watch you more closely than you may realize. They notice how you respond to frustration, how resilient you are and whether you're aware of your own feelings and the feelings of others. Never forget how much of a role model you are to them as they will probably copy a great deal of your own behaviours and reactions.

- Don't diminish the power of 'No'. Saying 'No' in the right circumstances is positive – it will give your children an opportunity to deal with disappointment and to learn self-control. To a certain degree (and hard though it is), your job as a parent is to allow your children to be frustrated and to work through it. Children who always get what they want aren't usually very happy.

- Speak to your children in an emotionally intelligent way. Say 'You seem angry' rather than 'You're behaving like an idiot'. When your children are whining or crying, saying something like 'You seem really upset' will always be a better option than simply telling them to stop.

- Encourage your children to think for themselves. When children are beyond their toddler years, you can encourage them to be more responsible. Instead of 'Put your coat on' you can ask, 'What do you need to be ready for school?' This helps them to develop confidence and responsibility.

- Encourage your children to be involved with day-to-day home life. Children who are involved in household chores from an early age tend to be happier and more successful because this makes them feel that they are an important part of the family. Try encouraging them with suggestions such as, 'You're such a good organizer, why don't you arrange the table settings?' or 'You're so good at making things neat, you can be in charge of tidying the playroom.' Children want to belong and to feel that they are valued.

- One of the most important things you can teach your child is respect. This is not the same as obedience, when children obey you only because they are afraid. When your child respects you, she will obey because she knows you want what's best for her. How best to teach it? Well, the best way to teach respect is to give it. When a child experiences respect, they know what it feels like and begin to understand how important it is. In showing respect, you will need to:

- be honest – if you do something wrong, admit it and apologize
- be positive – don't embarrass, insult or make fun of your child – compliment him
- be trusting – let your child make choices and take responsibility for the outcomes of those choices
- be fair – listen to your child's side of the story before reaching a conclusion about a situation
- be polite – use 'please' and 'thank you'; knock before entering your child's room
- be reliable – keep promises; mean what you say
- be a good listener – give your child your full attention (this can be hard with a chatterbox, but do your best).

Your opinion means a lot to your children. If you believe that they can succeed in what they want to do, they will believe they can as well. Encourage their independence. Give them responsibilities as soon as they can handle them. Help them to set and achieve goals. Their self-respect will shoot up when they see themselves achieving those goals. Most importantly, show love. Say 'I love you' often, and give plenty of hugs and kisses. If your child makes a mistake, reassure them that they are still loved more than anything in the world.

Summary

In this chapter you will have learned that by being a good role model to your children, as well as consistently teaching them the skills of EI, you will develop well-balanced young adults. In fact, if EI is new to you, you can develop your own skills through practising with, and learning from, your children.

- You can now incorporate the 'five basic steps' for developing EI in your children by using your own EI learning.
- You have learned that this hard work is worth the effort because it will impart skills to your children that will last them throughout their lives and give them an excellent chance of a happy and successful future.
- Whilst conflict is a fact of family life, you now have the skills to reduce it. Once you start using emotional coaching, you will feel yourself growing closer to your children. When your family shares a deeper intimacy and respect, problems between family members will seem lighter to bear.

- By following the advice in this chapter, you will also now be able to use EI skills to discipline your children in a (more) constructive way. When both you and your children are emotionally intelligent, you can assert a stronger influence. You will still be tough when toughness is called for. You will not be afraid to set limits or urge them to stretch themselves and do better. Because you have an emotional bond with your children, your words matter. They care about what you think. In this way, emotional coaching will help you guide and motivate children.

- You have hopefully understood that all this takes time. The psychological skills you give your child will not make a difference overnight. But if you work with them for several months, you will see a substantial improvement.

You will now hopefully be on the road to developing real EI in your children that will be long-lasting and that will benefit not only themselves but your family unit. One final word of warning, however. While parents can help their children develop into healthier, more successful adults, do take with you the understanding that emotional intelligence is by no means a cure for serious family problems that might require the help of a professional therapist. It also does not mean that all family arguments will cease, that there will be no more harsh words, no more bruised feelings, no more sadness or stress. Keep this in mind, and you will do very well in increasing family harmony and individual happiness.

> *We must remain as close to the flowers, the grass, and the butterflies as the child is who is not yet so much taller than they are. We adults, on the other hand, have outgrown them and have to lower ourselves to stoop down to them. Whoever would partake of all good things must understand how to be small at times.*
>
> Friedrich Nietzsche, philosopher and writer

EI is the habitual practice of using thinking about feeling and feeling about thinking, when choosing what to do.
Tim Sparrow and Amanda Knight, *Applied EI*, 2006

Emotional intelligence – not just the what, but the how

There is an abundance of definitions of emotional intelligence, and some are quoted here. Perhaps the easiest to appreciate is Daniel Goleman's idea that it is 'Just plain getting along with people'. To most of us, this is an important ideal that we constantly strive for, with all its rewards.

What this book has attempted to show you is how you acquire EI yourself. I would also like to place this 'how' in layperson's terms. EI requires you simply to step into another person's shoes, to see the world through their eyes. To do this, you will need to ask yourself questions such as:

- 'How would I feel/think about that if I were them?'
- 'What would I be saying if I were advising this person?'
- 'What are this person's wishes and hopes?'

You will start developing what I call 'other-awareness' quickly and easily. This is the basis for emotionally intelligent thinking.

Self-awareness requires open-mindedness. It means not only understanding and identifying how we are thinking and feeling, but being willing to expand our repertoire, as it were, asking questions such as:

- 'Are there any other ways I can look at this?'
- 'Does that thought really matter?'
- 'What might be the outcome(s) for me of thinking this way?'

Develop retrospective learning

One of the frustrations of attempting to make personal development changes is that, in the heat of the moment, we forget or are unable to recall quickly enough the new EI skills we are trying to acquire. Don't worry. This is fine. To move forward, simply apply retrospective learning until your brain can assimilate these new skills as its default. Retrospective learning means looking back at what happened and asking yourself 'What can I learn from this?' For example, if you felt that things went wrong – that you handled something badly, or the result wasn't what you'd hoped for – you can ask yourself 'What could I have done differently to get a better outcome?' Equally, whilst we often omit to do this, when something has gone well, it is good to look back at that too, and work out what you did that contributed to the positive outcome so that you can carry it with you into the future. To take this learning seriously, write your answers down on paper. This helps your brain absorb these new ideas more firmly. Spend time on this.

Exercise 61

To help your EI learning, replay a difficult situation in your mind. Imagine that what happened was recorded on a video recorder. Imagine yourself replaying the video – literally watching it on TV – but in slow motion this time, and notice the points at which you might have behaved differently. Take your time. Write down what you notice and see, and use vision to come up with a new way of dealing with such an event, should it reoccur.

Visualization

You can also plan ahead of time. Where there is something coming up that is important to you, where you want to achieve the best outcome and where you need to use your EI skills to their best, take the time to sit quietly and simply imagine this happening. You can start your visualization well before the event:

- Picture what you might decide to wear.
- Picture what you will be doing beforehand.
- Notice your environment – become really absorbed in where you are, and be able to picture it clearly.
- Move on to the moment you are thinking of where you wish to achieve your best outcome. If it is a conversation, picture what the other person will be looking like, how their demeanour might be, where you will be meeting – again, absorb the atmosphere in detail.
- If you are in a room together, notice pictures on the wall, the location of the furniture. Really *be* there.
- Now think of what you will do and say, and also what the other person is likely to do or say.
- Replay the visualization with a variety of different scenarios, and picture how you will deal with each of them.

Ideally, depending on the importance of the occasion, do this several times so that you feel that you have practised well and will be confident when the reality comes along.

You can use visualization for more general life goals too. Start to think about what you want from your life and your future and use visualization to imagine yourself both getting there and being there.

Visualization is a wonderful skill – used by many top business people and sports people when they picture themselves succeeding, which then makes the actuality both easier (virtual practice) and more likely (self-belief).

How to activate change

The people who get the most out of life choose to make the decision to take action that will result in change. Sometimes, external events, and the outcomes of those events, provide a catalyst that causes people to get started. For others, they cannot wait to become proactive, and it is more a case of understanding the right direction to go in. They simply decide that life can be better and feel determined to make that change. This is what you now need to do yourself.

Emotional intelligence is the ability to sense, understand, and effectively apply the power and acumen of emotions as a source of human energy, information, connection, and influence.
Dr Robert K. Cooper, *Executive EQ: Emotional Intelligence in Leadership and Organizations*, 1996

I hope that you now know enough about the positive benefits of EI to make similar choices. You have worked through this book so you are at least part of the way there. If you have not yet worked through the activities and exercises, note down those that you feel will be important to you, and that will make a difference.

> *Emotional Intelligence is a way of recognizing, understanding, and choosing how we think, feel, and act. It shapes our interactions with others and our understanding of ourselves. It defines how and what we learn; it allows us to set priorities; it drives many of our daily actions.*
>
> Freedman et al, *Handle With Care: Emotional Intelligence Activity Book*, 1997

If you can manage yourself effectively, then you will have no trouble becoming emotionally intelligent. You will understand yourself. You will have passion and a sense of purpose, and you will relate well to others, providing understanding, empathy and enthusiasm that will enable connection and intimacy.

Exercise 62

To help you assess your own competencies and those you would like to have, here is a summary of the well-researched key components of EI. Appreciate that every commentator has their own version of what they consider to be most important, and there is some flexibility here. Don't worry if you see slightly different lists in different books: it is often just a different way of saying the same, or a similar, thing.

Your goal is to assess those competencies that you consider you may already have, and highlight those that you may not have but would like to have, based on what you now understand of their importance, and the work that would be involved in achieving such skills.

Self-awareness	**Social awareness**
Emotional self-awareness	Empathy
Accurate self-assessment	Organizational awareness
Self-confidence	Willingness to help others
Self-management	**Social skills**
Self-control	Developing others

Trustworthiness	Leadership
Conscientiousness	Influence
Adaptability	Communication
Desire to achieve	Ability to generate change
Initiative	Conflict management
Building bonds	Teamwork

Adapted from Richard Boyatziz, 1999

In a nutshell, you are looking to achieve an ability to define your goals, be positively motivated to achieve them, maintain positive relationships with others and have good awareness of your personal strengths and weaknesses and how to harness these.

If your emotional abilities aren't in hand, if you don't have self-awareness, if you are not able to manage your distressing emotions, if you can't have empathy and have effective relationships, then no matter how smart you are, you are not going to get very far.

Daniel Goleman, psychologist and writer

Steven Covey defines the 'seven habits of highly effective people' in his book of the same name. These steps to success will automatically both develop, and hinge on, emotionally intelligent attributes. Check from the list below how well his suggestions dovetail with your own learning and development with EI. Write beside each habit which EI qualities Covey is asking the reader to draw on in order to develop the qualities he sees as important. I think you will find this quite easy to do now.

Be proactive. The habit of being proactive, or the habit of personal vision, means taking responsibility for our attitudes and actions.

Begin with the end in mind. This is the habit of personal leadership. Start with a clear destination to understand where you are now, where you are going and what you value most.

Put first things first. This is the habit of managing yourself, which involves organizing and management time and events.

Think Win:Win. Win:Win is the habit of inter-personal leadership. Win:Win is the habit of seeking mutual benefit. This thinking begins with a commitment to explore all options until a mutually satisfactory solution is reached (or to make no deal at all).

Seek first to understand, then to be understood. This is the habit of empathetic communication. Understanding builds the skill of empathetic listening that inspires openness and trust.

Synergise. This is the habit of creative cooperation or teamwork. Synergy results from valuing differences by bringing different perspectives together in the spirit of mutual respect.

Sharpen the saw. This is the habit of self-renewal. Preserving and enhancing your greatest asset, yourself, by renewing the physical, spiritual, mental and social/emotional dimensions of your nature.

> *If we lack emotional intelligence, whenever stress rises the human brain switches to autopilot and has an inherent tendency to do more of the same, only harder. Which, more often than not, is precisely the wrong approach in today's world.*
>
> Dr Robert K. Cooper, *Executive EQ: Emotional Intelligence in Leadership and Organizations*, 1996

You have emotional intelligence within you. It is there, at the ready. You simply need to become competent in activating it. You will. Good luck.

Suggested reading

Eric Berne, *Games People Play*, Penguin (1973)

Alan Carr, *Positive Psychology*, Brunner Routledge – the science of happiness and human strengths (2004)

David Caruso and Peter Salovey, *The Emotionally Intelligent Manager*, Jossey-Bass (2004)

Stephen Covey, *Everyday Greatness*, Rutledge Hill (2006)

HH Dalai Lama, *The Art of Happiness*, Coronet (1988)

Stefan Einhorn, *The Art of Being Kind*, Sphere (2007)

Melanie Fennell, *Overcoming Low Self-Esteem* (2002)

Daniel Goleman, *Emotional Intelligence: Why it Can Matter More than IQ*, Bloomsbury (1996)

Daniel Goleman, *Working with Emotional Intelligence*, Bloomsbury (1999)

Daniel Goleman, *Social Intelligence*, Hutchinson – the new science of human relationships (2005)

Professor M. Higgs and Professor V. Dulewicz (ASE), *Making Sense of Emotional Intelligence* (2002)

W. Robert Nay, *Taking Charge of Anger*, Guildford Press (2003)

Martin Seligman, *Learned Optimism*, Simon and Schuster – how to change your mind and your life (1998)

Martin Seligman, *The Optimistic Child*, Simon and Schuster (1996)

Lawrence Shapiro, *How to Raise a Child with High EQ*, Harper Collins (1998)

Websites

UK emotional intelligence testing

For critical reviews of EI testing, visit: http://eqi.org/eitests.htm

To take a test yourself, visit:
http://discoveryhealth.queendom.com/eiq_abridged_access.html

www.myskillsprofile.com/tests.php

http://psychologytoday.psychtests.com/tests/emotional_iq_r2_
access.html

There are no guarantees that these tests are meaningful, but you
may find them interesting.

UK emotional intelligence training

For a one day course, visit:

www.psychological-consultancy.com/training_emot_int.htm

For longer courses, visit:

www.summitconsultants.co.uk/consultant/emotional-
intelligence.asp

For distance learning or e-learning, visit:

www.trainingreference.co.uk/directory/emotional_intelligence.
htm

UK emotional intelligence organizations

Centre for Applied Emotional Intelligence (CAEI)

This is the representative body for professionally qualified
emotional intelligence practitioners in the UK and Europe.

www.emotionalintelligence.co.uk

British Association of Anger Management

www.angermanage.co.uk

British Association for Counselling and Psychotherapy

www.bacp.co.uk

To contact the author of this book, email:

chrissyw2@aol.com

index

teach yourself

life coaching
jeff archer

- Do you need your life overhauled?
- Would you like to be satisfied at work and home?
- Do you want strategies for long-term success?

If you've ever wanted to boost your confidence and set yourself new goals, **Life Coaching** is for you. It gives you direct, friendly motivation to review your aims, challenge your negative beliefs, and achieve fulfilment in all areas. It also provides checklists, case studies and all the practical resources you need to get where you want to be professionally, personally and financially.

Jeff Archer is a coach and director at Upgrade My Life, a life coaching consultancy that works with individuals and organizations helping them to reach peak performance. He is a regular contributor to a wide range of national media, newspapers and magazines.